D1741064

The Collected Poems of
William Nicholson
"The Bard of Galloway"

collected in a new and modern edition
with an introduction and biographical note

by John Hudson

ISBN 1 872350 77 1

The portrait on the front cover is of William Nicholson,
painted by John Faed R.S.A.

William Nicholson, born Borgue, Kirkcudbrightshire 1783,
and died there in 1849.

Published by:
G.C. Book Publishers Ltd
Wigtown
Scotland DG8 9HL

Tel/fax: 01988 402499
email: sales@gcbooks.demon.co.uk
web site: http://www.gcbooks.demon.co.uk

Printed and bound in Great Britain by
MPG Books Ltd, Bodmin, Cornwall

A Biographical Note

William Nicholson was born at Tanimaus, in the parish of Borgue, near the town of Kirkcudbright in Galloway, South West Scotland, in August 1783. He was the youngest of eight children. His father was a carrier, then a farmer and finally a publican in the town of Red Lion, today Ringford, four miles north of Kirkcudbright. His mother, we are told, loved to tell the young and apparently spoilt William stories beneath an old hawthorn tree, and in later life the poet credited his mother with inspiring his poetic gift. He was apparently a poor pupil, indolent and very shortsighted. We are told he attended Ringford school under the care of Mr. Kelly but other theories have searched for a mysterious pedagogue who may have inspired a precocious generation of Galloway writers from around this time. Mr. Heron of Borgue is a strong candidate. By the age of 14, Nicholson adopted the trade of packman, buying a stock of wares and travelling from town to town and farm to farm and generating a steady business, no doubt enhanced by his story-telling and affable personality. He was "extremely handsome, fully five feet ten inches high, with a most bard-seeming set of features". However, business was not all plain sailing and fluctuations in the market, especially in the price of muslins, frequently meant his trade ran aground. According to accounts he was also in the habit of taking time out in order to play the pipes or compose, and the conflict of interest between poetry and money remained with Nicholson all his working life, as it does with so many poets. In 1814 he managed to secure the publication of a volume of his poems and its success left him with a profit of £100. He invested it in muslin which promptly took a dive in value and the pedlar was back to square one. However, the book spread his fame and gained critical acclaim, so William Nicholson, the Bard of Galloway, was popular wherever he went. Success played upon his weaknesses and drinking became a severe problem. He began to see demons that conversed with him and gave him answers to major world problems. Armed with these, his poetry, and his writings on universal redemption (now apparently lost), the poet travelled to London to inform the King of what needed to be done to save the world. After being mugged and lost on too many occasions, a group of Gallovidians resident in London sent him back home. The Brownie of Blednoch was published in 1825 in the Dumfries Magazine and a second edition of his poems appeared in 1828. After this edition there is no clear detail concerning the poet's life. Some sources say he took up the life of a drover for a period. His friends say that they knew little of him in the last fifteen to twenty years of his life. M. M. Harper states that "for some years before his death the harp of the bard had been unstrung, and little was known of him beyond the bounds of his native parish, saving that he was leading a 'quiet, reflective, exemplary life'". He died at Kildarroch, Borgue, on 16th May 1849 and he is buried in the churchyard of Kirkandrews, by the Solway Firth. An inscription on the stone set up by his brother John contains the lines, "No future age shall see his name expire".

Introduction

One hundred and fifty years ago William Nicholson died. It had been twenty-one years since the printing of the second edition of his poems, an edition that didn't include his greatest poem, "The Brownie of Blednoch". His friends, in the latter years of the poet's life and with an eye on posterity, wished Wull, as he was known, to put his work in order. They feared that much that was valuable would be lost. It probably was, for William Nicholson equated scholarship with pedantry and lived day to day. Ironically, many of Nicholson's posterity-conscious friends are recorded solely because of their association with a man who could hardly be bothered to inspect the proofs of his first edition. There was no collected edition, nor has there been until this one.

Two editions, essentially the same, appeared during the second half of the nineteenth century, and a 'new' edition, which in fact is the same as editions three and four but in a leaner format, appeared in 1914. These three editions since Nicholson's death are incomplete, excising many poems from editions one and two and omitting some hand-written pieces, perhaps because the editor, M. M. Harper, did not know of their existence (see below: A note on previous editions). Since then, the star of "The Bard of Galloway" has declined and the memory of his most famous poem, "The Brownie of Blednoch" has become the preserve of a generation who committed his poetry to memory but who are now almost all gone. Therefore, this edition is the first that can lay claim to achieving anything like the wish of Nicholson's immediate circle of friends and admirers during his lifetime. If Nicholson could be consulted upon this enterprise, I imagine he might smile, wish it luck, shrug his shoulders and move on. But why is a poet of stature left to fade, almost from awareness altogether, especially in a country that prides itself on its letters?

Nicholson addresses an oral tradition even more than Burns, whose shadow across Galloway and Ayrshire has certainly put many nineteenth century poets in the shade. He found it difficult to take the notion of literary posterity with any seriousness. The few anecdotes around his life (there is no reliable biography) paint a somewhat contradictory picture of a half-blind, avid reader who hated scholarship and loved gossip. Despite his apparent eagerness to read, he couldn't spell, nor had a full grasp of grammar and needed an amaneunsis to record his poems. Yet we are told he corresponded in his own hand and wrote fine prose. All this is remotely possible but the men who are telling these stories (and in fact it could well be one person regurgitated) are clearly members of the nineteenth century middle class that belong to a different social milieu from that which Nicholson frequented. When they refer, for example, to Nicholson's lack of learning they mean he had no classical learning. Nicholson, however, worked by ear and by a hand-me-down imitation, transmuting the raw material of folklore and popular issues through story telling, music making and singing, into his own, recognisable style. Recognisable, that is, to the rural, land-dependent men and women on farms and small communities throughout Galloway; the written form of the poems that are, inevitably, contained in this book show evidence of many different literary re-modellings. One poem might be in Gallowegian, another in Scots, another in English; some might use what has become known as the apologetic apostrophe while others use "ing" and "of" quite happily. Such variation almost certainly depends on the literary predilections or circumstances of the scribe. These poems, therefore, are like photographs taken on different cameras by photographers of varied skill that capture a scene for a moment but, by virtue of their means, crop away the rest of the world around them. Such re-modellings would not have concerned Nicholson because he would have reworked his poems and songs according to his location and state of mind.

An interesting case comes in the form of a previously unpublished poem, "The Blacksmith o Blednoch". There are two handwritten versions in different hands in the library of artist E.A. Hornel at Broughton House, Kirkcudbright, now in the care of The National Trust for Scotland. They seem to involve much guesswork. Malcolmson's version states it was transcribed from Nicholson's hand which was "illegible throughout" and confesses to the "assistance of my own muse" when he was transcribing the poem. It was certainly written up during Nicholson's lifetime, although its author seems not to have assisted the process. The other, anonymous, version is in the same hand as the scribe of another rediscovered Nicholson poem written on the coming of age of the Earl of Selkirk in 1830. Either one or probably both "correct" Nicholson's metre by removing an "and" here or a "but" there, changing a dancing anapaest into a sturdy iamb, or changing the word order or phrase order in a line so that the colloquial becomes the lofty. Both attempt to tone down the sexual content of the poem by dropping a line at a vital point in order to preserve at least some of the female protagonist's virtue. These scribes had learning and used it to transform the energy of a land-based culture concerned with confronting its hopes and fears through its storytellers into drawing-room respectability. Of course, they preserved the poems for us today.

Earlier mention was made of the passing generation that can still recite the "Brownie of Blednoch". I have heard it recited from memory, and it was recited not only in Galloway but also in Ireland. Its popularity, even today, when there are few who can recite it, is mythical. Yet later nineteenth century editions of

7

Nicholson's poems didn't run to more than a few hundred copies, were distributed across a wide area (Glasgow, Edinburgh and London, as well Wigtown, Kirkcudbright and Dalbeattie) and sold by subscription. They were hardly, from the production standards, the property of poorer folk. It is the poorer folk, however, who can remember "The Brownie". Is it possible that the versions of "The Brownie" that you can still hear on a Wigtownshire farm today are versions handed down through the generations since Nicholson sang it for his food and keep as he travelled the countryside selling wares from Ayrshire to the Borders? Perhaps the oral tradition is still alive and potent. Local primary school projects on folklore and local history must also play a part in this process of preservation and re-interpretation. Teachers may well have recited the poem to their classes until quite recently, although a stricter curriculum seems to have banished "The Brownie" today.

To get closer to Nicholson it is necessary to address the mythologising of the poet's life by his commentators. The picture of the rude poet touched by genius, inspired rather than learned, not only sounds far too like Burns and Hogg to be entirely believable but reflects the inner tensions of the educated middle classes of the time. It therefore has to be seriously questioned in relation to the truth about Nicholson, the man and poet. John MacDiarmid, Nicholson's biographer for the second, 1828 edition, at one point in a rambling and yet sometimes revealing essay, invokes the name of Rousseau so unselfconsciously that he might as well have been invoking the authority of the Bible. Nicholson is made to fit the gospel according to eighteenth century idealism. We end up with a list of strange contradictions which reflects the nineteenth century intellectual's attempt to reconcile nature with learning. It was an uneasy partnership that led, in the worst instances, to opinionated moralising and a condescending misrepresentation of a rural, land-dependent culture that could never grasp the bourgeois aspirations of the French Revolution. Hence we are told that due to his short-sightedness Nicholson could not become a shepherd despite the fact that there is no suggestion he might ever have become a shepherd even if he had twenty twenty vision. His elder brother became a respected publisher in Kirkcudbright, his father ended his days as a publican; why should Wull count sheep, except that being a shepherd was in accord with the idealist models of the time? We are told that he rejected education and this explains the lack of wit or classical knowledge in his work. This overlooks the carefully handled conceits, which are very difficult literary devices that frequently occur in his work. He rarely makes classical references but he was performing to an audience for whom classical allusion would not have had much meaning. As Nicholson writes of the Priest in "The Country Lass",

> "He spak o darts, and Cupid's bow:
> Neist cad her Venus, Heb, and Iris,
> And names that stunned her wi their queerness-"

The people's supernatural world was of "brownies, bogles, ghaists and wraiths"; they were real and not abstracted personifications of natural or moral powers. We are told that Nicholson liked nothing more than to sit by a stream and read, and that he was zealous and possessed of a genius inspired by adversity. A few paragraphs later this is cited as evidence for a lack of commercial drive - another paramount concern in the nineteenth century. We are then told that Nicholson couldn't write or only rudimentarily, based on the phonetic model. The interpretation suits the commentators for our poet was, as fits the model, educated by nature. One is reminded of Burns presented to Edinburgh society as the natural man, a myth that still persists to this day. It shows the inability of such commentators to understand the soil in which Nicholson grew and it is a difference of perspective that, because of its association with wealth, academic learning and the printed page, has nearly condemned a whole tradition.

But there are more tantalising guesses about the real Nicholson that come from the intuitions of the local folk, and not from their "betterers". Nicholson was not alone in Galloway, not even in Borgue where he was brought up, in his passion for poetry and song. In fact, Galloway was in something of a "literary" renaissance at this time, producing many now largely forgotten poets, some of whom equal Nicholson in different ways, and offer Scotland a resource yet to be brought to the public's attention. James Mactaggart (1791-1830), author of the remarkable "Scottish Gallovidian Encyclopaedia" (1824) and a poet, was born an easy walk from the Nicholson household. John Gerrond (1765-1832), David Davidson (active 1789) and Samuel Wilson (1784-1863), were among many others in Galloway at the time. Joseph Train (1779-1852), Walter Scott's informant was a local writer in his own right, author of "The Wild Scot of Galloway", published by John Nicholson, William's brother, in 1840. The Cunninghams, also contemporaries, were local to the wider region, as was Dr. Alexander Murray, an unremarkable poet, but a highly respected academic and advisor and friend to Nicholson. Revealingly, the sister of James Hogg (1770-1835) lived on the Tongland Road, just north of Kirkcudbright, not a few hundred yards from where the Nicholson family once lived and by which anyone entering Kirkcudbright from the north would have to pass. There are letters from Hogg to the Kirkcudbright poet, inn keeper and Nicholson scribe, Malcolmson (1793-1848) in which Hogg refers to his family and there is little doubt that he visited his sister. Hogg helped Nicholson get his first edition published. MacDiarmid, who clearly works on a great deal of hearsay and doesn't seem to know Nicholson personally that well, refers to Nicholson meeting Hogg in Edinburgh. He surely did, but it seems sensible to suggest that Nicholson and Hogg met in Kirkcudbright? Nicholson would have known all these characters. In his travels to raise subscribers for his first edition he succeeded in getting over fifteen hundred names!

The point is that the literary culture of Galloway during Nicholson's lifetime was remarkably rich and busy. It was a largely oral tradition changing rapidly to a written culture that was, by the second half of the nineteenth century, to preserve and ossify that tradition into parrot-fashion Burnsiana. We don't need models supplied by the Enlightenment to explain and ultimately obscure the genius of Nicholson, we simply need to look at what was happening in Galloway at the time. However, today, to fully see that picture there is much restoration work that needs be done. Collecting the works of William Nicholson is one step on a long journey towards revealing a Scotland that may change the way we look at ourselves and clear away the varnish of foreign intellectual models and of a later nineteenth century obsessed with bogus images of Scottishness, Robert Burns included. Such work can achieve what has long been the felt need that lacked a means: reveal new layers of cultural richness to go alongside the images that Scotland thrusts at the tourist market.

This edition, therefore, is the best that can be done at the moment. It is not a monument cast in bronze but a half-accurate record of the quixotic genius of a poet who is partly lost and partly transformed. There is little doubt that Nicholson became a drinker, and it has been suggested that his output declined once he became prompted by his demons and theories of universal redemption. There are statements that he fell on hard times and became a dependant of the parish but no record has turned up of him on the poor roll. There is a story of him denouncing his greatest poem "The Brownie of Blednoch" in his later years for it has "nae moral". He is reported to have said this after a lively recitation before the Rev. George Murray (1812-1881), a fellow poet. The story is echoed in "The Country Lass" but there it suggests that Nicholson had been criticised for his refusal to moralise.

> "Now, should some critic snap and snarl
> At this lang tale, without a moral..."

Maybe he said it, maybe he felt he should say it before a Minister, or maybe the culture that felt great poetry showed great moral purpose said it for the vagrant drunkard who never said "thank you" but whom everyone liked.

In the end we are left with the works as they have come down to us. They range from simply wonderful to the pedestrian. "The Country Lass" has definite literary pretensions and was written at the prompting of Dr. Murray while Nicholson's poetry was in preparation for publication. Rumour has it that four lines of "The Country Lass" are by James Hogg. Many aspects of the poem are revealing but its insight into human character, as every commentator agrees, is profound. Indeed its probing of human hopes, aspirations and foibles rivals Jane Austen. As it is written in four beat rhyming couplets it also reveals something of the aural tradition from which Nicholson's art springs. Nearly every couplet rhymes perfectly in the voice of the Stewartry of Kirkcudbright, or more accurately, the

Parish of Borgue, from which Nicholson comes. Read it in any other Scots and the rhymes will often seem half rhymes. The beat, too, may seem thumpy or unvaried. On the page, yes, but not in the mouth of a local to Nicholson's Galloway. Although "The Country Lass" was never designed to be performed, its art is the art of the live storyteller.

The songs, many of which were still sung into this century around Dumfries and Galloway, have now almost died out. Their quality is patchy but they evidently suffer at the hands of various scribes. At their best they are lyrically sublime and open heartedly revealing. M. M. Harper, in his later editions excised some of the better pieces, probably because they were either too topical or too unaffected, honest or near the knuckle. They reveal another aspect of Nicholson the poet, showing a bleak despair that doesn't fit the image of jolly Wull to whom disaster was like water off a duck's back. One such piece is "Song", set to the tune of "Bonny Dundee". I wonder if there isn't a strong autobiographical element here. "Where are the joys that I felt in life's morning?" asks the opening line. It takes us until the end of the fourth verse of seven to discover the cause of the grief and the fact that the griever is a woman. She mourns the loss of her "Willie", Nicholson's name. The poem quickly returns to the subject of despair. As a conventional loss poem it spends a long time dwelling on abstract misery. If, however, we exchange the grieving woman of convention for the mature poet, and see Willie as the young Nicholson, the personal meditation takes on a very modern darkness.

One is reminded of the way Burns in verse or Schubert in song could take conventional models and materials and make them into something special. Did Nicholson attempt this? Again the scribe interferes but read that poem as an older man's address to lost joy and the nihilism has a personal tone that disturbs where a more conventional piece would merely draw sympathy. Certainly Nicholson and his contemporaries such as Mactaggart were aware of the trends of the time and would use them to popularise their work. The subject of the woman abandoned by a lover once she is pregnant travelled the length and breadth of the island. Clare uses it as do Mactaggart and Nicholson, frequently. They address contemporary issues. War left many women with a child or children to bring up on their own. The poet is always on the woman's side. Maybe they found sympathy for the stigma and quality of being an outcast. Their condition, socially and psychologically finds a brother in the poet that wrote "Fortune, I fear not thy smiles nor thy frowning,/ Nought can now move me on this side the tomb!" Indeed, the theme of the outcast is so strong in Nicholson's work that we are forced to ask questions about his life and social status. The Brownie, Nicholson's greatest creation, is very much an outcast; Sandy, the hero in "The Country Lass" is only accepted back into society through a lucky inheritance, and "Lines on Seeing a Poor Old Man Shunned at a Sacramental Occasion" contrasts the "thoughtless, proud and gay" with the wretched outcast whose only rest is with God. How much of this is autobiography?

A drinker, a converser with demons, peripatetic pedlar and poet, a warm lovable man, an acute observer of his friends' foibles, his life crossed the paths of thousands of folk. He upset people because of his apparent ingratitude but he seems to have had that universal gratitude that rarely singles out individuals for recognition. Mactaggart, in his Scottish Gallovidian Encyclopaedia, does not have an entry under Nicholson but under Wull, for he knew that anyone in Galloway who would look up information about one of its greatest poets would know the man by that familiar name. He says, "every body is fond of him, his

cracks are extremely diverting, so humourous, yet so melan-
choly...". He closes his article, "And should all mankind desert
him, I hope he will find me never far away; whatever I can do for
the good of that man, so shall it be. If I have a saxpence in the
world, a part of it be his, and a word to spare, let that be said in
his favour".

Forty-nine years after the poet's death "a large and
representative committee" met in Kirkcudbright on 1st October
to agree a suitable site for a memorial to mark the fiftieth year
of the poet's death. It was unanimously agreed that Borgue
village, five miles from Kirkcudbright, would be the most
suitable location, and that a sum of £250 needed to be raised by
subscription. The Committee consisted of many prominent
figures including Nicholson's editor for the later editions, Malcolm
McL. Harper from Castle Douglas and his publisher Thomas
Fraser from Dalbeattie; George G.B. Sproat from Gatehouse of
Fleet, himself an enthusiastic poet, and artists associated with
Kirkcudbright, T.B. Blacklock, originally from Kirkcudbright,
then resident in Edinburgh, William Mouncey, who once owned
the house in which this introduction is being written, W.S.
MacGeorge and, most famous of them all, E.A. Hornel of
Broughton House, Kirkcudbright, who took inspiration for
many of his works from Nicholson, including a famous work on
the Brownie of Blednoch now in Kelvingrove, Glasgow. The
memorial was executed by W. H & J. Newall of Dalbeattie and
the sculptor was Mr A. McF. Shannon of Glasgow. The image
was derived from a portrait executed during Nicholson's lifetime
painted by John Faed, a Gatehouse of Fleet born Royal Acad-
emician. On 18th August 1900, Sheriff Andrew Jameson,
unveiled the memorial. Nicholson's fame was set in Dalbeattie
granite and gradually, ironically, people stopped reading his
poetry.

Alongside all the complex social issues that go towards this decline, Scotland tends too readily to be seen as a "one poet country", not only by outsiders but the Scots themselves. Moreover the themes Nicholson treated: betrayed love, frustrated love and the consolations of nature or the failing of such consolations in old age are no longer the concern of "high art". His love interest belongs more to the world of the pop song. Nature has been tamed or failed us through science and is largely the consolation of the retired class. His satires are just as sharp but satire's references date. The element of gothic horror maintains a niche in the interest of the public and will always do so but it is Nicholson's concern with the supernatural Brownie that still captures the popular imagination. In a letter written to the editor of the Dumfries and Galloway Courier upon the occasion of Nicholson's death in 1849, a correspondent comments that the Brownie of Blednoch "entitles its author to a remarkable status", and that the poem "has been seldom surpassed in what is called graphic power". He concludes that "it is, in short, second only to the 'Tam o' Shanter' itself". John Brown, another commentator, goes further, "here is the indescribable, inestimable, unmistakable impress of genius. Chaucer, had he been a Galloway man, might have written it, only he would have been more garrulous and less compact and stern."

There is, however, a lot more to William Nicholson than the Brownie of Blednoch and upon the one hundred and fiftieth anniversary of his death another memorial is fitting. If one enjoys signs and omens then the times augur a revival. The date of his death, the 16th May, is exactly the same as the "birthday" of Scotland's Book Town, Wigtown, a date the town aims to celebrate every year. Wigtown is next door, quite literally, to Bladnoch, the village of the Brownie of legend and of the newly transcribed poem "The Blacksmith o Blednoch". As we move into a new century and a new millennium we have the prospect of a new Scotland with its parliament set to address Scotland and Scotland's culture. Perhaps, most significantly of all, we have a resurgence in the literary arts in Galloway the likes of which has not been seen since those days when William Nicholson toured the region.

Recite these poems, sing them if you know the tunes or invent new tunes for them. I hope this volume brings enjoyment to many and keeps the memory of William Nicholson alive for some years to come.

A note on previous editions

The 1814 edition was entitled "Tales in verse and Miscellaneous Poems descriptive of Rural Life and Manners by William Nicholson". It had a quote from Hogg on the frontispiece, "plain his garb and plain his lay". It was published in 1814 in Edinburgh and sold in Edinburgh, Dumfries, Kirkcudbright, (through T. Macmillan) and Wigtown. The second, 1828 edition was printed in Dumfries and points of sale were in Glasgow, Edinburgh, Dumfries and in Kirkcudbright, this time through Nicholson's brother, the printer John Nicholson. In the west of the region the focus had moved to Newton Stewart. The third edition came out in 1878 and was edited by M. M. Harper. This left out many poems from the previous two editions and was the first time "The Brownie of Blednoch" had been collected. The Brownie first appeared in the Dumfries Magazine in October 1825. The fourth edition is the same in nearly all respects as the third and came out in 1898. The final edition to appear before this edition, came out in 1914 and is in content the same as those of 1878 and 1898.

A note on this edition and on punctuation and authography

Contrary to previous editors I have chosen not to organise William Nicholson's poems into categories such as song, tales, satires etc., but opt for the simple principle of alphabetical organisation ignoring "the", "a" and concentrating on the first strong word of the title. I have done this for several reasons. Firstly, previous editors don't entirely agree on how to subdivide Nicholson's work. Secondly, the divisions applied in the nineteenth century do not seem as relevant today as they might have done then. Finally, such division involves very partial decisions. The Brownie, for example, was set to music. Does that make it a song? It is a story. Is it therefore a tale? No principle seems adequate, hence the very arbitrary notion of an alphabetical one.

I have also simplified indentations and layout to be in line with modern presentation, cutting out large drop capitals and the like. If layout seemed vital to the poem's purpose or meaning, I have retained it. I have also chosen not to include a glossary of Scots terms. I do not expect a dictionary to be printed at the back of every book I read that is in English, and Scots dictionaries are now commonplace.

I have brought this edition in line with current printing in Scots and abandoned what has come to be known as the apologetic apostrophe, which seems an appropriate editorial decision in many ways. Thus meanin' becomes meanin, o' becomes o, wi' becomes wi, ha'e becomes hae and i' becomes i, etc. I have also removed apostrophes from grammatical constructions that imply an English grammatical context although Scots is being used. Thus the past participle of fa becomes fan and not fa'n for the apostrophe implies the English fall/fallen construction. In certain cases the apostrophe helps clarify meanings as in een and e'en where the first is Scots for eyes and the second is a poetic contraction for even or evening. All apostrophes indicating poetic contractions are retained, for example "believ'd"

Nicholson, as has been remarked, required a scribe. Depending on whoever wrote down his poetry we find many variations in typography and variations from edition to edition. Some poems are written in a language close to English, employing "ing" endings and hand instead of han, for example. These I have left unchanged but poems on similar themes are often not only in Scots but in Gallowegian Scots. Perhaps Nicholson, like the balladeers, changed his voice to suit his audience but we have no way of knowing whether this is true and anyway the printed version more likely reflects the personal considerations of his scribe. This is borne out by the differences noticeable in the two versions of the "Blacksmith o Blednoch" that have come down to us. Some poems pose greater problems for they mix languages in what might be described as a confused unselfconsciousness. I have not undertaken to rationalise these oddities for we have no indication from the poet as to what line to adopt and they do not spoil our appreciation. Other fraught issues are spelling, accents and, in the longer poems, the use of paragraphs. The earlier printed editions carry varied spellings from poem to poem: hazel becomes hazle, for example. To interfere seemed more pedantry than usefulness and it would continue the process of systematisation that has buried Nicholson's genius beneath a mound of corrections. Accents that indicate a sounded syllable occur in either an accute accent or a diaeresis over the final e. I have left these as they appeared in earlier additions, although any pronounced difference seems, to me, dubious. The way paragraphs are used, in for example "The Country Lass", will seem strange to many readers. Whether it was Hogg, Nicholson or the printers that chose this layout is unknown but to alter it would not, in my opinion, help matters at this stage.

I have few qualms over putting Nicholson's Scots poems in the language he spoke to the folk of Galloway's towns and farms. It makes for a tidier page, something a contemporary audience appreciates and, I hope, will appeal to a new generation of Nicholson readers. On the eve of a new Scottish parliament, it seems in keeping with the times to record this poet's work in his own tongue but with twentieth century orthography. Scotland is fortunate to possess three indigenous languages: Scots, Gaelic and English, as well as playing host to many others. I believe that as readers progress through this book Nicholson in Scots will become natural and obvious.

John Hudson, Kirkcudbright, 1999.

THE EDITOR

John Hudson is a poet, editor and critic who lives in Kirkcudbright. Born in London in 1958, he moved to Galloway in 1987 after periods spent in France and Orkney. In 1995 he founded, with several friends, Markings, a magazine dedicated to literature and the arts. He is a founder member of the poetry performance group, "The Solway Festival Poets" and frequently reads his poetry in public. His poetry has been published nationwide and frequently anthologised and 1996 saw his first collection, Medusa Muse. His short film, "Wednesday's Girl" was shown at the 50th Edinburgh International Film Festival. He writes a weekly arts review column in The Galloway News and runs an extra mural poetry class for the University of Glasgow, as well as organising arts and literary events, including the Kirkcudbright Arts Festival and the birthday celebrations for Wigtown, Scotland's Book Town, in 1998. He has undertaken extensive research into the poetry of South-West Scotland and edited a selection, "Round About Burns" in 1996 for the Stewartry Museum Service. A selection of the poetry of physicist James Clerk Maxwell appeared in 1997. In 1999 he was awarded a Scottish Arts Council writers' bursary in order to work on his next collection.

Contents

Annandale Robin
Tune "*Woo'd and Married and a*"

Young Robin had been at the market,
And hired himsel wi Craigfast;
Forbye the wee drap in his noddle,
Had got a the wages he asked.
He wha had been touned out wi tenants,
Would soon be head man to the laird -
A point at baith shearin and mawin,
And bigg a the ricks i the yaird.

      It's right aye for lads to live canty,
      And lasses, till they get a man;
      For fouks to be social and sober;
      And aye as content as they can.

The moor-hags were wide - but he sten'd them,
He staptna for stick nor for stane;
Till down by the scroggs o Congailly,
He met bonny Bet a her lane.
Ae luck on the back o anither:
He lang wished her kindness to seek;
Nae scene could be sweeter for wooin
What time was he fitter to speak?

      It's right aye for lads to live canty, etc.

"Stay still, tell us where ye've been daundering -
For me I hae been at the town;
See sic a braw knowe there forenent us,
Would maist tempt a saint to sit down.
Hech me! but it's lang since I saw ye,
And vow! ye're grown gaudy and grand;
The chiels will sae pester and plague ye,
For peace sake ye maun tak a man."

It's right aye for lads to live canty, etc.

But Bet lookit blate like and bashfu,
She sighed and said naething ava;
Hung her head - rowed a strae round her finger,
Gart Robin aye closer to draw.
He prest her, he courtit, he clappit,
Snapt a kiss, for it weel on was dark
When, to crown a his hopes in a hurry,
She haflins said aye in a hark.

It's right aye for lads to live canty, etc.

Aye lyin ane's lane soons grows dowie;
Sae Robin thought lang for a spouse;
Farewell to the freaks o the market,
The lang wage and braw gentle house.
The auld fouks were couthy and kindly,
The bridal was hurried aff han;
Sae kindly's they cuddled thegither,
But houses, or haddin, or lan.

It's right aye for lads to live canty, etc.

But wha can tell how things may alter,
Or what a half-year brings about;
For Robin turned dowffer and duller,
As Betty began to speak out.
She cries out for this thing and that thing,
Like a bell through his lug her tongue twangs;
And aye siccan matches she might haen,
While he sits as dumb as the tangs.

It's right aye for lads to live canty, etc.

The Auld Man's Address to Health*

Come, lovely Health, wi laughin ee,
I lang thy rosy lips to pree;
To wanton in thy glowin arms,
And revel o'er thy heaven o charms -
Thy smile each fear and care disarms.

In vain would wealth her pearlins heap,
Or varied year her treasures sweet;
What boots proud honour twined wi fame?
Thine is the substance - theirs the name;
Even love, but thee, grows dull and tame.

'Tis thine our fondest hopes to draw,
And sweeten Nature's beauties a;
To crown afresh the warrior's head,
And strew wi joys the bridal bed,
Where virtuous love and truth are laid.

The second edition has "Old" for "Auld" in the title

'Tis thine the poor man's peace to earn,
Wi thrivance to each dauted bairn;
Bear up the burden o his toil -
His dark and lonely thoughts beguile,
And deck cauld poortith wi a smile.

Wilt thou within my woodland's dwell,
"A bloomin like thy bonny sel?"
Or paint afresh my Peggy's cheek,
Where nature did her wark complete,
Now treacherous Time has wasted bleak?

The violet blossoms by the broom;
The bean-field blaws its saft perfume;
The wild-rose sheds its dewy tear
The cuckoo sings her sang fu clear -
And a to gar thee linger here.

Well do I mind in blythe se'enteen,
When light the dancers skipt the green
Thy artless presence graced the place,
And men'd the tints on every face,
But chief my.Peggy's modest grace.

When wark was scant and bairns were sma
And life's dull plough was dreich to draw;
Thou then wast ever smilin near,
And proffered hopes o future gear,
And dang out dull forebodin fear.

Full forty springs hae slippet by,
Since Hymen's han the knot did tie -
Thou ne'er hast left us lang distrest,
Except to show wha loed the best;
But wha could judge the kind contest?

But now, alas! thy smiles are seen,
Like angel's visits, far between;
As birds of passage, fleet and gay,
Flit from bare bush to flowery spray,
Thou leav'st wan age to grope its way.

Ill fares the wight that's left by you,
In lonely bield wi comforts few;
Or totterin, forced to seek his bread,
Through the wide warld without a shed,
Wi no a friend his cause to aid.

Virtue and Youth are twins wi thee -
Alas! were they sic friens to me!
The latter lang, alas, has left me!
O mony a joy she has bereft me;
Oh! may the first, through Hope, infeft me.

The Banks of Dee
Tune *"Roof o Straw"*

The purple morn o'erspread the sky,
    The day-star shewed his head;
A reverend ruin nodded nigh,
    With waters round it spread.
The bird of night had ceased her tale,
    And fluttering fled from me;
As softly sighed the morning gale,
    Along the banks of Dee.

The bended lilies lined the banks
    Around the fishes' bed;
And trees in gay and motley ranks,
    Sloped out the flowery glade.
The glossy blackbird on the bough,
    Sang to his mate with glee;
And joined the lark, yet wet with dew,
    Upon the banks of Dee.

Here rustic labour wets his scythe
    And sets his edge with care;
The humming wild-bee leaves his hive,
    To sip the flowerets fair.
The merry milkmaid gaily sang -
    Her bosom light and free;
While listening echoes joined alang,
    The winding banks of Dee.

Here, too, Dame Nature's handmaid, Art,
        Had reared her arches gran,
Of bridges rare beyond compare,
        On noblest Doric plan.
The shielded mansion half I viewed,
        That pleased the passing ee;
And clustering villages were strewed,
        Along the banks of Dee.

Peace to your scenes, my native plains,
        Where plenty ever spreads!
May truth and honour crown your swains,
        And beauty grace your maids.
Let rural mirth and pity's sigh,
        Still in your breasts agree;
And fellow-feeling still be nigh,
        Around the banks of Dee.

The Banks of Fleet
Tune "*O'er the Muir amang the Heather*"

I sing the bonny banks o Fleet,
        Where Nature spreads her various treasure;
Frae fruits and flowers of every hue,
        To berries blae, and craps o heather.
Thy pebbled shores and sea-girt isles,
        Thy far-famed woods and views sae mony;
Thy hills and towers where simmer smiles,
        Thy strappin lads, and lasses bonny.

Thy winding banks and flowery dells,
  With bloomin fields around in order;
Where commerce spreads her flowin sails,
  Auld Card'ness towers o'erlook thy border.
Upon thy banks a borough stands,
  Sae feat and healthy, few's completer;
If search through Scotia's southern strands,
  Nane's shieled sae biel, nor shows aught sweeter.

Castramon waves his leafy locks,
  Amidst the meads where flowers are springing;
And shields wi woods his furrowed rocks,
  Where lightsome birds are blythely singing.
The Rusco ruins, nodding grey,
  Where Gordons gay ance blythely ranted;
And wild woods spreading o'er the brae,
  By nature's ruleless hand been planted.

At distance Cairnsmuir rears his form,
  The hoary snaw his haffits wrappin;
His dark brows brave the wintry storm -
  A blue mist bonnet coers his tappin.
Fain would I sing each noble name,
  Where kindness blends wi wealth her traces;
But deeds surpass the poet's pen,
  As native smiles do borrowed graces.

Fareweel, ye bonny banks o Fleet,
  Where nature spreads out a her treasure;
Frae fruits and flowers o every hue,
  To berries blae, and craps o heather.

The Banks of Tarf
Tune "*Sin my Uncle's dead*"

Where windin Tarf, by broomy knowes,
Wi siller waves to saut sea rows;
And mony a greenwood cluster grows,
And harebells bloomin bonnie, O.
Below a spreadin hazel lee,
Fu snugly hid where nane could see,
While blinkin love beamed frae her ee,
I met my bonnie Annie, O.

Her neck was o the snawdrap hue,
Her lips like roses wet wi dew;
But oh! her ee o azure blue,
Was past expression bonnie, O.
Like threads o gowd her flowin hair,
That lightly wantoned wi the air;
But vain were a my rhymin ware
To tell the charms o Annie, O.

While smilin in my arms she lay,
She whisperin, in my ear did say,
"Oh! how could I survive the day,
Should ye prove fause, my Tammie, O?"
"While spangled fish glide to the main,
While Scotland's braes shall wave wi grain,
Till this fond heart shall break wi pain,
I'll aye be true to Annie, O."

The Beltan winds blew loud and lang,
And ripplin raised the spray alang;
We cheerfu sat and cheerfu sang,
The banks of Tarf are bonnie, O.
Though sweet is spring, when young and gay,
And blythe the blinks o summer's day;
I fear nae winter cauld and blae,
If blest wi love and Annie, O.

The Blacksmith o Blednoch

There are two handwritten transcriptions of this poem. The right hand page is Malcolmson's version, while on the left is an attempt by an anonymous scribe. I have included both versions for it demonstrates well the difficult process of transforming an orally presented work onto the page.

Whar Blednoch roun green hills doth wind,
Leas his rude rocks an his moors behind;
Whare yon lowly tree, wi its branches twa,
Hangs quivering o'er the mouldering wa;
Whar the dull night wren delights to cry
At the weary traveller passing by.
There lived o yore, as I've heard said,
An honest limb o the blacksmith trade.
What though the fiels wi their flowers be braw,
An bluidy man's fingers grow roun the wa;
Yet it's lonely an still, an the heart finds pain
To pause on the days that are past and gane.
What rout; an what revel, what cracks hae been here,
What ploughman assembled wi broken gear,
In shepherd's gray frae their hills sae wide
An discussed half the news o the country side.
An here were seen some fleysome sights
By the hinds that were late on the market nights -
Unsavoury saunts, an unhallowed lights,
An eldritch scraichs, wi wild hahas,
While the sparks flew round like fiery bas.
For some powerfu wight got his bellows to roar,
Till the red hot coulters flew out at the door:
Syne unearthly chaps knocked on pell mell,
'Twas thought that the deil was turned blacksmith himsel.

An leas his rude rocks an his moors behind;
Whaur lonely trees wi branches twa,

And the dull night wren delights to cry
At the weary traveller passing by.-
There lived of yore, as I've heard said,

But what though the fields wi their flowers be braw,
An bluidy man's fingers grow o'er the wa;
It's lonely an still, an the heart finds pain
To pore o'er the days that are past and gane.
What routes, what revel, what cracks hae been here,
What ploughman assembled in broken gearin broken gear
Wi In shepherds in gray, frae their hills sae wide
Discussing the news o the country side.
And, here hae been seen some fleysome sights
By them that were late on the market nights -
Unsavoury scents and unhallowed lights,

Till the red hot couters flew out at the door:

Likes the deil had turned blacksmith himsel.

A this is affirmed, in our present times,
To be true as the maist that is published in rhymes.
On yon brae-side that the streamlet has worn
Whare nought is seen but a serried thorn,
Wha's back is sair bared by the winds o the west
Whare the chattering piet has bigget her nest,
A bien farm steading ance stood there,
An the farmer had daughters baith good an fair;
'Twas said that for marrying they a were inclined,
Had they met but wi matches to suit their mind.
Now our smith had nouther wife nor wean,
His father was frail, an his mother was gane,
Afore he grew dowie wi lying his lane.
For his cousin Kate, a maiden fu light,
Came oure to cook, an keep a things right;
But her paws grew hard an ane blackened his shoon,
Her meltiths were cauld ere her jobs were done;
Sma thrift was made, an sma wabs were spun,
An some trifles were lost that could never be foun:
Sae he thought wi himsel, an he thought nae wrang,
For the weather was cauld, and the nights were lang,
That friens are oft fremit, an seldom take care,
While a wife wad be cautious o wasting your ware.
Now the farmer's first daughter, I think they cad Jean,
Was a tosie young lass wi twa twinklin een.
What though she was na the gimp lady make,
And the sun had been sair on her face an her neck;
Yet something o gracefuness sat one her brow,
And merriment circled the shape o her mou.
Than she spak ay sae saft when ye met her her lane,
That wha saw her but ance wist to see her again.
Now she thought on a day, as she sat at her wheel,
How her shoon wad be best to be done at the heel;

To be true as maist that is put in rhymes.
    On yon braeside that the burn has worn
Whare nothing grows but a serried thorn,
Whas bark is sair bared by the winds o the west

A bien farm ~~house~~ steading ance stood there,
An the farmer had dochtèrs gude an fair
'Twas said that to marry they baith inclined
Had they met but ~~wi~~ matches to suit their mind.
    Now our smith had neither wife nor wean,
His father was frail, an his mither was gane,

But her paws grew hard and black's his shoon

An some trifles lost that couldna be foun

That friens are oft fremit and tak sma care
While a wife wad be cautious o wasting ware.
    Now the farmer's first daughter, they cad her Jean

What, though she was na, the gimp lady make,
And the sun had been hard on baith face and neck;
Yet a something fu gracefu sat on her brow,

And she spak ay saft when ye met her lane,

Now she thought one day, as she sat at her wheel,

For in thae days the lasses wore a hie-heeled shoon,
Ans she thought she kend best how she wanted them done.

Sae through to the smith had she straight gane away,
As light an as blithe as the bird is in May.
He dighted his dark brows frae stoure an frae sweat,
An flung by a shoe that was bent the first heat;
For wha can be slow when the lassies entreat?
Nae doubt but he did them wi caution an care,
An rasped an filed till his shoulders were sair;
But lo! in the midst o their winks an their jokes,
The day darkened dreadfu, wi loud thunner shocks:
The blue lightning flashed its dread terrors roun,
And the low'ring clouds poured a deluge down;
While aghast an trembling stood the maid,
But the son of Vulcan was undismayed
An ay she drew nearer, an ay she said
She wondered he wasna far mair fleyed.
He took her to house - wi her back at the wa
She sat till the tempest wad cease to blaw,
An look'd an leant - then he did say
You kend your need that cam out sic a day.
When the murky south began to clear,
The bosom o Jean was divested o fear
The sun glanced out wi a glorious light,
An the gloff swiftly fled frae fore his sight;
So Wellington came, so the Frenchmen flew
At the well-sung battle o Waterloo.
The lassie was wistfu in gathering her shoon,
To cross the ford ere the flood came down.
The smith came down to the nether well howe
To tak fareweel, an to see her through,
But the water was leaping frae brow to brow.

In thae days the lassies wore a highheeled shoon,
And she thought ~~she kend how she wanted~~ them done.
    on a way she would like
Sae through tae the smith she straight gaed away,

  He dichted his dark brows fae stoure and fae sweat,
An flung bye a shoe that was bent the first heat;

Nae doubt but he did hers wi caution an care,

But lo! in the mids o their winks an their jokes,
The day darkened dreadfu, wi loud thunder shocks.

And the lowering clouds poured a deluge down;
While aghast and trembling with fear stood the maid
~~But~~ The bauld son of Vulcan was quite undismayed
An ay she drew nearer an ay to him said
She wondered he wasna far meikle afraid.
He took her to his house - wi her back to the wa
She sat still till tempest wad cease to blaw,
An looked and leant, then to her did say,

  When the dull murky south began to clear,
The bosom of Jean was divested of fear

And the gloff swiftly fled frae before his sight;
As when Wellington came and the Frenchmen flew

To bid her fareweel, an to see her through,
But the water was lipping frae brow to brow.

He saw by her looks that her heart was in grief,
Yet wat na weel how he could gie her relief;
An fain wad persuade her to gang back,
To stay a night till the spait wad slack,
But she blushed and said how the folks wad taulk.
She sighed and said, what will be done,
The sorrow light on you baith for shoon!
But the smith spak out, since ye winna wait,
This is no time to fyke and prate:
Already, I fear, 'tis past your power,
The sky again begins to lower;
An syne that I'm langer in limbs than you,
Come on my back, an I'll bear you through.
I waive ilk maiden modest joke,
An a the persuasion that brought her about,
To bless his back wi sicken a lift -
O Love! thou art never without a shift.
Nor need I tell what transports past,
When first she clasped him hard and fast
Around his neck, an roun his waist -
It was na the chill o the water guest,
Or the foolish fear o them baith being drowned,
That racked his brains, an his nerves sae stunned;
But it was a feeling o purest glow,
That mortals here are allowed to know.
What though the saucy waves been dashed,
Yet stoutly her through wi his burden swashed:
An when he had reached the farther green,
A prouder pedlar was never yet seen;
An what though her tongue nae accents spak,
As down she slept frae aff his back,
Yet there was a look, an there was a smile,
That well repaid him for a his toil.

Yet, wat he nae weel how to gie her relief
He fain wad persuaded her to gang back
An stay a night till the spait wad slack,
But she blushed and said how folks wad taulk.

There is a time to fyke and prate:

The sky is again beginning to lower;

We'll waive ilk maiden modest joke,

Nor need we tell what transports past,

It was na the chill o the water ghaist,
Or the foolist fear o them baith being drowned
That racked his brains and nerves sae stunned;

What, though the saucy waves sore dashed
Full stoulty her through wi his burden swashed:
An when he had reached the further green,

An what though her tongue nae accents spak;
(*this line is missing in second MS*)

'Twas now the time his suit he prest -
His arm was slipped around her waist
Then sat them down by the elder tree,
That shielded the pair frae ilk prying ee.
The storm was past, the evening was still;
The sun was sinking behind the hill;
The blitter was harping his hollow bassoon,
An the sheep frae the fells were wearing down;
But little deemed they as they sate in the shade,
How the time had flown by, an the water was spread,
That seldom afore had been sae big,
An nae sic a thing in thae days as a brig.
'Tis said they agreed, an wha coud them blame,
She saw that the laddie coud na won hame,
When a the lave were fast asleep,
That they wad best to the corn-mow creep,
For to them sic lodging an leisure were sweet.
(*this line is missing in the first MS*)
An wha o us wad think it mean,
If we coud then meet wi our ain dear Jean.
'Twere vain for me to further explain
What sayings were said, an what vows were taen.
The breathings o lovers but badly tell,
An uninterestin to a but themsel:
But soon in the morn the floods were faen -
The smith his fire gey early had blawn;
For strong was his arm and sicker his chap -
The smoke spued out at the chimla tap.

His arm was slipped around her waist.
They sat (*in margin*)
An it shielded the pair frae ilk prying ee.
The storm was past, the evening still

How ~~the~~ time had flown bye, and the water spread;
For it ~~That~~ seldom before had been ever sae big

That as a the lave were fast asleep,
They twa had best to the corn-mow creep,
For to them sic lodging ~~and leisure were~~ sweet
Where time after time their lips did meet.

If we could thus meet wi our ain dear Jean.
It were vain for us to further explain

The breathings o lovers we canna weel tell
An are no meikle interest to aught but themsel

The smith gey early his fire had blawn
And ~~For~~ strong was his arm and sicker his chap
While the smoke spued out of the chimney tap.

The Braes of Galloway
Tune *"White Cockade"*

Oh! Lassie, wilt thou gang wi me,
And leave thy friens i south countrie -
Thy former friens and sweethearts a,
And gang wi me to Gallowa?

    Oh! Gallowa braes they wave wi broom,
    And heather-bells in bonnie bloom;
    There's lordly seats and livins braw
    Amang the braes o Gallowa.

There's stately woods on mony a brae,
Where burns and birds in concert play;
The waukrife echo answers a,
Amang the braes o Gallowa.

    Oh! Gallowa braes, etc.

The simmer shiel I'll build for thee,
Alang the bonnie banks o Dee,
Half circlin roun my father's ha,
Amang the braes o Gallowa.

    Oh! Gallowa braes, etc.

When Autumn waves her flowin horn,
And fields o gowden grain are shorn,
I'll busk thee fine in pearlins braw,
To join the dance in Gallowa.

    Oh! Gallowa braes, etc.

At e'en, when darkness shrouds the sight,
And lanely langsome is the night,
Wi tentie care my pipes I'll thraw,
Play "A the way to Gallowa."

    Oh! Gallowa braes, etc.

Should fickle fortune on us frown,
Nae lack o gear our love should drown;
Content should shield our haddin sma,
Amang the braes o Gallowa.

    Come, while the blossom's on the broom,
    And heather-bells sae bonnie bloom;
    Come, let us be the happiest twa
    On a the braes o Gallowa.

The Brownie of Blednoch

There cam a strange wight to our town-en,
And the fient a body did him ken;
He tirled na lang, but he glided ben
  Wi a dreary, dreary hum.

His face did glare like the glow o the west,
When the drumlie cloud has it half o'ercast;
Or the struggling moon when she's sair distrest.
  O sirs! 'twas Aiken-drum.

I trow the bauldest stood aback,
Wi a gape and a glower till their lugs did crack,
As the shapeless phantom mumling spak,
  "Hae ye wark for Aiken-drum?"

O! had ye seen the bairns' fright,
As they stared at this wild and unyirthly wight,
As he stauket in 'tween the dark and the light,
  And graned out, "Aiken-drum!"

"Sauf us!" quoth Jock, "d'ye see sic een;"
Cries Kate, "there's a hole where a nose should hae been;
And the mouth's like a gash which a horn had rien ;
  Wow! keep's frae Aiken-drum!"

The black dog growling cowered his tail,
The lassie swarfed, loot fa the pail;
Rob's lingle brak as he ment the flail,
  At the sight o Aiken-drum.

His matted head on his breast did rest,
A lang blue beard wanered down like a vest;
But the glare o his ee nae bard hath exprest,
    Nor the skimes o Aiken-drum.

Roun his hairy form there was naething seen,
But a philabeg o the rashes green,
And his knotted knees played ay knoit between:
    What a sight was Aiken-drum!

On his wauchie arms three claws did meet,
As they trailed on the grun by his taeless feet;
E'en the auld gudeman himsel did sweat,
    To look at Aiken-drum.

But he drew a score, himsel did sain,
The auld wife tried, but her tongue was gane;
While the young ane closer clasped her wean,
    And turned frae Aiken-drum.

But the canny auld wife cam till her breath,
And she deemed the Bible might ward aff scaith,
Be it benshee, bogle, ghaist or wraith -
    But it feart na Aiken-drum.

"His presence protect us!" quoth the auld gudeman;
"What wad ye, where won ye - by sea or by lan?
I conjure ye - speak - by the Beuk in my han!"
    What a grane gae Aiken-drum!

"I lived in a lan where we saw nae sky,
I dwalt in a spot where a burn rins na by;
But Ise dwall now wi you, if ye like to try -
    Hae ye wark for Aiken-drum?

"I'll shiel a your sheep i the mornin sune,
I'll berry your crap by the light o the moon,
And baa the bairns wi an unkend tune,
    If ye'll keep puir Aiken-drum.

"I'll loup the linn when ye canna wade,
I'll kirn the kirn, and I'll turn the bread;
And the wildest fillie that ever ran rede
    Ise tame't," quoth Aiken-drum!

"To wear the tod frae the flock on the fell -
To gather the dew frae the heather bell -
And to look at my face in your clear crystal well,
    Might gie pleasure to Aiken-drum.

"Ise seek nae guids, gear, bond, nor mark;
I use nae beddin, shoon, nor sark;
But a cogfu o brose tween the light and dark,
    Is the wage o Aiken-drum."

Quoth the wylie auld wife, "The thing speaks weel;
Our workers are scant - we hae routh o meal;
Gif he'll do as he says - be he man, be he deil,
    Wow! we'll try this Aiken-drum."

But the wenches skirled "he's no be here!
His eldritch look gars us swarf wi fear,
And the fient a ane' will the house come near,
    If they think but o Aiken-drum.

"For a foul and a stalwart ghaist is he,
Despair sits brooding aboon his ee bree,
And unchancie to light o a maiden's ee,
    Is the grim glower o Aiken-drum."

"Puir slipmalabors! ye hae little wit;
Is't na hallowmas now, and the crap out yet?"
Sae she silenced them a wi a stamp o her fit;
    "Sit yer was down, Aiken-drum."

Roun a that side what wark was dune,
By the streamer's gleam, or the glance o the moon
A word, or a wish - and the Brownie cam sune,
    Sae helpfu was Aiken-drum.

But he slade aye awa or the sun was up,
He ne'er could look straught on Macmillan's cup;
They watched - but nane saw him his brose ever sup,
    Nor a spune sought Aiken-drum.

On Blednoch banks, and on crystal Cree,
For mony a day a toiled wight was he;
While the bairns played harmless roun his knee,
    Sae social was Aiken-drum.

But a new-made wife, fu o rippish freaks,
Fond o a things feat for the first five weeks,
Laid a mouldy pair o her ain man's breeks
    By the brose o Aiken-drum.

Let the learned decide, when they convene,
What spell was him and the breeks between;
For frae that day forth he was nae mair seen,
    And sair missed was Aiken-drum.

He was heard by a herd gaun by the Thrieve,
Crying "Lang, lang now may I greet and grieve;
For alas! I hae gotten baith fee and leave,
    O, luckless Aiken-drum!"

Awa! ye wrangling sceptic tribe,
Wi your pros and your cons wad ye decide
'Gainst the 'sponsible voice o a hale countryside
    On the facts 'bout Aiken-drum?

Though the "Brownie o Blednoch" lang be gane,
The mark o his feet's left on mony a stane;
And mony a wife and mony a wean
    Tell the feats o Aiken-drum.

E'en now, light loons that jibe and sneer
At spiritual guests and a sic gear,
At the Glashnoch mill hae swat wi fear,
    And looked roun for Aiken-drum.

And guidly folks hae gotten a fright,
When the moon was set, and the stars gied nae light,
At the roaring linn in the howe o the night,
    Wi sughs like Aiken-drum.

The Butterfly and the Bee
A Fable

A gaudy butterfly that sat
Upon a flaunting tulip's lap;
While from its tubes of crimson hue,
He sipt the virgin morning dew;
His tinsel wings waved by his side -
His chiefest beauty and his pride -
Bedropt in Nature's fancying hours,
Vied with the beauties of the flowers.
The star of day, from ocean's breast,
Rolled up the portals of the east,
And shone afar o'er lakes and streams,
To glad creation with his beams.
The heath-bell blue adorned the wild,
And flowers within the garden smiled:
The fluttering insect thus elate,
While cringing reptiles round him wait,
Like fops, when blest with pride and treasure,
Think all things form'd for their pleasure.
Shall then his deeds of fairest hue,
Be hid and not exposed to view;
He flaps his wings, he hummed aloud,
And thus addressed the wondering crowd
"Behold in me, of high descent,
A traveller of great extent;
A connoisseur of noble parts,
Adept in sciences and arts:
The eglantine and woodbine bower,
I have survey'd in my tour;

Cowslips, carnations, I have trode,
And made the violet my abode:
When zephyrs waked my soft repose,
I dined upon the honied rose,
And revelled on the scented pea -
For all the flowers were fond of me.
My soaring wing hath dared to fly,
Up to yon towering pear-tree high;
Or perched alone, unfeared of fall,
Upon the lofty garden wall;
Nor stopt I there, till objects new,
Again attract my wondering view.
A spacious sea, extended wide,
The circling billows lashed the side,
Where living mountains stemmed the flood,
And cackled to their giant brood;
A cloud-topt tower, where thunder rings,
Monsters both with, and without wings.
All these and more, myself did brave,
That ye poor creepers can't conceive: -
But surely ye'll allow the charge,
That I have viewed the world at large"
A sober snail, of slowly pace,
That on a leaf lay stretched at ease,
In all his life that scarce had seen
Above a cabbage or a green,
Yet deemed they yielded dainty store -
Because he ne'er had dreamt of more -
Hearing the bully boast aloud,
His dangers thus by field and flood,
Dire discontent his bosom seized,

And envy all his vitals heezed:
His body round in grief he wreathed,
While thus his woe and wants he breathed:
"Ah! cursed fate - ah! captious Nature,
That formed me such a clumsy creature!
My footless form thus keeps me here,
Through all the beauties of the year
Till piercing winds, or driving snows,
Cut short my life and end my woes.
Oh! had I but the towering wing
Of yon gay flutterer of the spring,
I should not loiter here alone,
Alike unknowing and unknown."
A busied bee, with humming noise,
That o'er her labours did rejoice,
Hearing at large the lengthened tale
Of empty butterfly and snail,
A conscious ardour filled her breast;
She thus the butterfly addrest:
"Vain, empty, ostentatious worm,
That no instruction can reform;
Nor sage experience with her light,
Can ever guide thy views aright,
But like the crowd that always change,
Thou lov'st the marvellous and strange;
Though thou hast roamed o'er flower and field,
What hidden truths hast thou revealed;
Or sound conclusions, drawn from nature,
Of use to thee or other creature.
Even now, while summer's sun doth shine,
Thou, idly gadding wast'st thy time;

And with thy follies dost foment,
The bursting sigh of discontent,
Through all the simple creeping tribe,
And fill'st their itching minds with pride.
I, too, have traversed all thy rounds,
And e'en o'erleaped thy largest bounds;
Toiling, with pleasure, for my hive,
To keep our commonwealth alive:
But small's the all that we have viewed,
And short's the path we have pursued.
Again, when winter chills the day,
My store shall well each toil repay,
When thou in dust shalt low be laid,
And all thy transient beauties fled."

Our fable ends; and you no doubt,
Can easy find the moral out:
For trifles far we need not roam -
There's Butterflies eneu at home.

Complimentary Verses to the author of The Thistle, a song on the fate of the Stewarts

Peace rest in thy dwelling, thou true Son of Song,
That sing'st by the banks of the Cree;
Thou strik'st the bold numbers, thy grey rocks among,
And sweet sound thy harp-strings to me.

Thus lofty and lonely still let thy notes rise,
And tell of the times that are past;
They soothe the lone bosom in secret sighs,
Like the wild-passing sound of the blast.

I see Caledonia descend in her car,
Thy brows to encircle with bays;
Tho low lies her crest, like yon dim-setting star,
Her "Thistle" shall live in thy lays.

The Country Lass
A Tale in Eight Parts

Part 1
The Introduction

In yon ha house, ayont the fell,
Whar rural peace and pleasure dwell;
And waning age, and wanton youth,
And modest worth, and simple truth,
There lived a lass, if Fame speak true,
Wi laughin een and cherry mou,
And sweeter charms than I can paint:
In face and form without a taint.
Her father's name was John Mclellan -
Douce honest man, he farmed a mailin;
In youthfu days wrought for his bread,
Wi gude blue bonnet on his head,
And though the times began to mend,
His auld acquaintance aye he kend;
Blest wi a rive o common sense,
To polished life made nae pretence:
Was simply plain in a his dealins,
Nor wad he step aside for mailins:
Ne'er preed anither but his wife, -
Ne'er heard a law court in his life;
Could tak his chappin, pay his kain,
But never tippled by his lane.
Nor wad his wifie waste his winnin,
But kept a feat wi her ain spinnin -
Held aye the house baith tight and bein,
And made their meltiths warm an clean:
Whan winter nights war dark and lang,

Could tell her tale or lilt her sang,
'Bout deeds o weir in former days,
Or lovers' dools on Scotlan's braes,
Wi weirds and witcheries aft atween,
And unco sights that some had seen;
Nor was she backward or unheedfu
To ken, or tell o things mair needfu -
Had read the Unconverted's Call,
And learnt hail loof-breads o St Paul,
Wi sic like learnin as was common
For ony couthy, country woman.
    But wha can read the buik o fate?
Although his sonsie helpmate Kate
Was aye the apple o his ee,
And mony a bonny bairn had she:
Though fickle fortune brought them gain,
I wot they warnae free frae pain:
For death, the terror o us a,
That thins the cot and weeds the ha,
Stauks furth wi a his darts and scythes,
In shape o measles, kinks and hives,
Till only ane their care did claim,
And bonny Betty was her name.
    Ere saxteen simmers o'er her flew,
She could baith card and spin the woo
Row up the fleeces at the clippin,
And had the milkness a in keepin -
Could knit and sew, and a sic wark,
As dress her faither's Sunday sark,
Crimp up ilk ruffle, frill, and border,
And set the tea-cups a in order;
And maxims mony mae were taught her,
That ilka mither shaws her daughter:

Was kind and blythsome wi her kin,
Or ony neightbour that cam in;
For chapman chiel or beggar body,
Her weel waled word was aye fu ready,
Till a, baith far and neare confest,
She was the bonniest and the best.
    Now, as sic lasses are aft scant,
O sweethearts routh she didna want:
Sic beauty, and the name o siller,
Gart wooers flock like wil-geese till her.

Part 2
The Farmer's Son

The first, a farmer's eldest sin,
Was beef without, but blank within:
On market Mondays sauld a stirk,
On Sunday closely kept the kirk,
Wi pious zeal, and future views,
To wale a wife, and catch the news.
I wat a pleugh he weel could tune,
And trim his graith, and mend his shoon:
Could shear a point baith fast and slaw,
And thresh, and dike, and ditch, and maw;
But then his een and thoughts were blind
To beauties o the heart and mind.
It never crossed his brain the smallest
If Rome or Glasco town was aul'est,
Was Enbro yont or neist the Forth,
If France lay east, or west, or north:
Unmoved, "The Waes o War" he'd hear,
Nor piteous tale could draw a tear:
In vain the spring her flow'rets spread,

Thoughtless, he'd on the daisy tread;
In vain the wee birds happ'd and sang
The buddin hazle bank alang;
Or lamkins roun him skipt an play'd,
While ewies for the younglins maed:
Sic sights nae pleasure brought ava -
Only, if every ewe had twa,
If grass wad gar the outlers sell,
And how the braird look'd on the hill.
At vulgar jest or smutty sang,
His vacant laugh was loud and lang:
Proud, without prudence, wit, or wealth,
His only property was health -
He saw at least ae specious charm -
The lassie's gear wad stock a farm;
And though his hopes did highly shore him,
'Twas but sma kindness she had for him.
        It chanced ae morning mirk wi mist,
He saw young Betty ere she wist,
Ca'in the ewes wi cannie care,
That war a scattered here and there:
Aff ilka blade the dew-drap flang,
As light she through the clover sprang.
A hunder beauties flushed her cheek,
Her risin bosom seemed to speak:
The napkin loosed, wi ease he saw
The bonniest keams o new-faun snaw.
'Twas then that Love played him a shavie,
And strak his dart in donsie Davie.
Her coats war kiltet to the knee,
And shawed right shapely to the ee,
A leg sae handsome, feat, and clean -
She leuk'd like ony fairy queen.

But what made him sae simply sober,
To see the lass amang the clover,
And gart his heart aye thump and pat,
Though neither fley'd, nor cauld, nor wat,
And start behint a buss and cour,
Though he had seen the lass afore,
And silent lie like ony maukin,
Wha ne'er afore was feared for talkin,
Till ewe and lamb had left the lair,
And she was hame, and he was there?
　　Neist time was at a countra waddin,
When baith were present at the beddin;
On bride cakes sweet they chewed the cud,
The drink gaed roun in merry mood,
Wiss'd routh o bairns and happy days,
And poured libations mang the claes:
The left leg hoe they now prepare,
And circle roun wi anxious care,
To see wha fortune wad decide
To be the neist bridegroom and bride: -
When lo! the die of fate was cast,
And lightet saft on Betty's breast: -
The shouts o laughter roun were spread;
She stepped aside, but naething said;
While Davie thought the time's at hand
That he maun either fa or stand.
　　O Happiness, ye wily jade,
That maks baith poor and rich sae mad,
And towering genius dull and doited,
And sober sages capernoited,
Wha anxious search but canna get ye,
While ye sit still and never fret ye:
Though aft your secret dens and haunts,

Are fund by folks wha are nae saunts.
By thymin second-sighted skill,
I've fund the mansion whar ye dwell;
For 'deed ye're seldom sicker set.
'Tis when the piper's martial lay
Sweeps o'er some Highland wild strathspey;
Whar sprightly flickering dance is seen,
And lightly flows the tartan sheen;
A reekin bowl, or Highland gill,
The ready rhino at our will;
A frien at hand wi wit and glee,
The lass we like best on our knee:
Wha winna be content wi this,
Is ill to please o wardly bliss.
      Yet still our wooer wasna happy,
Though fully half and half wi nappy;
Though hale and feir, and routh o rents
Like Adam still he had his wants;
Alas! he kentna whar to gang -
But Davie saw his help at han.
Right blythe he sat by her, I ween,
But ithers soon thrust in atween,
And if she on them deigned to look,
He thought it something frae him took;
For envy catched him in her thrall,
And turned his sweetest joys to gall.
But whisky aye gars courage come,
Dispels ilk doubt, ilk fear and gloom;
For first ae service, then anither,
His courage syne began to gather.
He eed his boots, and thought them braw,
Then a his fears he flung awa;
He bowed - she smiled, and raise to reel,

And few could play their part sae weel.
Her lint-white locks were belted roun
Save curls that played her ee aboon,
Where Cupid was in ambush laid,
And mony a wily trick he played:
Her shapely neck, o fairest hue,
Was graced wi garnets, gilt and blue;
But vain wad Art her gum-flowers shaw,
Whar Nature's lilies rival snaw.
    He gazed, he viewed her o'er and o'er,
Nor lap he e'er sae light afore,
Syne pud her down upon his knee -
O, what a happy man was he!
He hoasts for breath, but naething said,
His han upon her shouther laid.
His hopes were high, his heart was fain,
He dights his brow and hoasts again:
Yet still in art o wooing slack.
At length she gloomy silence brak:
"How's a your fouk at hame?" quo she;
"They're middling weel," again quo he;
"To set ye hame I wad be fain;
Ise warrant ye'll no gang your lane.
I saw ye brawlie when ye cam
Out owre the muir wi gard'ner Tam.
As soon as ye cam to the brow,
I lookit lang and thought 'twas you.
Our young cowt goved, I ga'em a whack,
He pranced and syne the back-rape brak.
When I was tackin't up thegither,
He ate the brecham aff the ither:
For he's sae fu o pranks and tricks,
And jumps, and flings, and snores, and kicks.

Yet thought he's ill and ill eneugh,
I ne'er saw ony in a pleugh,
When rivin through yon bent and heather,
That I wad gie the tane for t'ither.
But though I say't that soudna tell,
Nane e'er dare work wi'm but mysel.
My mither o him dreads aye skaith,
And says he'll some day be my death.
And ance he hurt my shin right sair," -
Thinks Bess, "ye'll mak a bonny pair!"
So up she gat and tripped her ways,
And left the laddie in amaze.
Nae langer could she thole his blether,
But slip't hame canny with her faither:
He ne'er again, at kirk or fair,
Durst ever wi her taigle mair.

Part 3
The Kirkless Priest

The neist was o the black coat tribe,
Wi sturdy limbs and shouthers wide
Uninfluenced by cauldrife Saturn,
Had lang been gaping for a patron;
Yet somehow ne'er the nail could hit,
But mist it ay just at the bit.
Whether the age had swarmed wi teachers,
Or men were thowless grown 'bout preachers,
Or sense was scorned while clubs had chances,
Or priests war plentier grown than manses,
Or if the laddie wanted merit,
Or savoured mair o flesh than spirit,
Or gin they're a like ither men, -

It's mair I'm sure than I can ken.
　　　　But wha can hae a mind sae mirk,
Although his reverence gat nae kirk,
To think that he should jog through life,
Without the pleasures o a wife;
Or like a celibastic Roman,
Forswear the joys o a lovely woman!
A neibour's bairn was he, I ween,
And at the college aft had been;
Had learnt to trim his beard wi grace,
Wi whiskers half-gate o'er his face;
Could speak and spell wi modish skill,
And broach the doctrine o "free will";
Put on his claes wi meikle pain,
And brush them clean o stour and stain;
Name kittle words as smooth as satin,
And shaw how they were born frae Latin;
White whalebone busks for ladies dink,
And wrote love-letters without ink:
Right sharp the vulgar's fauts discernin,
And saw the benefits o learnin;
Could mak a bow or shake a paw
Wi ony gentle o them a.
　　　　When dark December days were short,
He sometimes tried the shooting sport.
Now as John's groun was thinly dyket,
And had the muirfowl that he liket,
He's aft come in, and tak a seat,
To see the lass, and crack wi Kate,
Or gie the present o a hare; -
For he was ay made welcome there,
To what the house could e'er afford
O coal, or yill, or bed, or board.

Syne she would speir gif he could tell
What age was Adam when he fell?
Whether the serpent flew or gaed?
If Abel's wound was on his head?
Gif Cain's mark was warl like?
Wha bigget Paradise yard dyke?
Wha it was first that span a sark?
Gif Aaron's rod was peeled o bark?
If circumcision hurt ane sair?
What was the weight o Abs'lom's hair?
Wi mony mae o sic like kin,
Might puzzlet mony a learned divine,
Wer'tna that Stackhouse, by his study,
Has made them pat and plain already.

     When for sic kindness, in return,
He'd aft invite them owre the burn,
And fell twa birds whiles wi ae stane -
Said grace and saw young Betty hame.
When times would answer, now and than,
He'd tak her kindly by the han,
Say, not a lady he did know,
A han sae saft or fair could show;
Then kisst and clasp it to his breast,
And say he would be truly blest,
The too much favoured happy man,
Would get that heart as weel's the han;
While she would, laughin, push him aft,
And say, I'm sure the man's gane daft.

     When last frae Enbrugh he cam hame,
He brought her a braw muntit kame,
A box, a brooch, a gowden pin,
And learnt her how to put them in;
Then shawed her fashion's newest rig,

And how to crisp and curl a wig, -
Wi meikle mair, ye needna doubt,
A countra lass kent nought about;
Till through the countra, kirk, and clachan,
She turned the tap and ton o fashion.
      But ance, when gloamin shed her rays,
As they cam owre the bracken braes -
The auld folks now were out o sight,
The sun was sunk ayont the height, -
His arms he laid around her waist,
And ay he close and closer prest.
"My dear Eliza! love," he said,
"My only angel! heav'nly maid"
Come, sit thee down, till I explain
The causes o my grief and pain.
With ardent fires my breast doth burn,
It's a for your sweet sake I mourn.
O let me clasp thee in my arms,
And bless me wi thy heaven o charms."
Syne said his heart was in a low;
He spak o darts, and Cupid's bow:
Neist cad her Venus, Heb, and Iris,
And names that stunned her wi their queerness;
Till, by some motions o his hand,
She better cam to understand.
'Tis love," says he, "maks me sae free;
I hope, my soul, ye will forgie."
"These hopes shall ne'er be realised!"
Quo' Bet, offended and surprised.
"Is that your Scripture, and your readin,
Your Enbrugh tricks and college breedin?"
Yet still he held her in his grip,
And wasna willin to let slip

Says, "Haud your tongue, Bess, for my blessin,
David, ye ken, was gien to kissin."
When lo! a bark cam frae the hill,
And syne a whistle, loud and shrill.
'Twas Shepherd Sandy, wi his doggie,
Cam skelpin down the glen sae scroggie;
His plaid out-owre his shouther flung,
While wi his notes the echoes rung.
Right fain was she the tyke to see:
The fribble down upon his knee;
Nae langer parley did he claim,
But let her gae, and slippet hame;
Nor was he anxious to come back,
Wi Kate or her to get a crack.
     Oh! luckless, perverse, nameless failin!
Tacket to every rank and callin,
To a capacities thy lessons
Addressëd are, and a professions.
Alike thy baleful influence clings
To cobbler's stalls and courts o kings;
Thou lead'st the righteous aft astray,
The virgin green and maiden gray,
Till scarce a lifetime can atone
For what some thoughtless moment's done.
But if thou meanest to do right,
Or I've found favour in thy sight,
Oh! never saw thy wil-kail seed
Near by the poet's houseless head,
Or let his dreams ken aught about ye,
Alas, he's fraiks enow without ye.

Part 4
Sandy the Shepherd

Now Sandy was a clever chiel,
And could baith read and write fu weel;
Had thoughts on things baith in and out -
Kent mair than ony herd about:
At sic like wark as he profest,
Was never hinmost, if no best.
He ance a day could dance and sing,
And on the pipes play mony a spring.
But love, the bane o high and low,
That shoots the shepherd and the beau,
Had hurt his peace, but ment his pen,
Although he ne'er let ony ken:
For Poverty, wi iron claw,
That cauldrife rook that paiks us a,
Had chilled his hopes and dimm'd his views:
He for a helpmate woo'd the muse.
Nature, through a her varied hue,
To him had charms for ever new.
He aft would sing his lassie's praise,
Wi a his native burns and braes,
And link them up in rustic rhyme,
To answer his loud chaunter's time:
Or sing, in rude and bolder lays,
Some follies o our modern days.
But where the social band was met,
He ne'er was seen to gloom or fret,
'Twas there he herriet pleasure's nest,
And couped his cap up wi the best,
Till, saft and clear, like morning dew,
The flights o wit and humour flew.

Or if a frien did stand in need
O help by either word or deed,
He ne'er was sweir a han to len
And deemed it siller's noblest en;
That gart himsel whiles be negleckit,
And by the warldly disrespeckit.
     But Betty whiles would guess a part, -
For love by looks can judge the heart.
They baith were bairns brought up thegither,
And aye were unco pack wi ither.
When at the school he took her han,
Or cleant her claes if she had faun;
And wi his plaid would screen the show'r,
Ere love to plague had catch'd the pow'r.
When she to milk the ewes had gane,
He cam and bure the leglen hame;
Or at the bught she ne'er thought lang,
While he tauld o'er some tale or sang;
And lent her buiks to read at leisure,
Syne talk'd them o'er wi meikle pleasure,
Till words and thoughts begat a kinship
O ties mair tender far than frienship.
     But Kate saw soon, wi wily ee,
And thought that sic things shouldna be;
Their bairn taen up wi a herd laddie,
And cootlan by their lanes already.
So she was now kept close within;
Her mither aye had tow to spin,
Till love and learnin a gaed way.
At the neist term, ne'er asked to stay,
He hired him wi a neibour man,
And saw but Betty now and than.
     Sae it was a but fair and right,

That he should see her hame that night;
Jocosely spier'd whar she had been,
That she was gaun sae late at een;
And how the priest had chanced to turn
Afore he saw her owre the burn?
She hid her face, and tried to laugh,
And said, "She hadna been far aff:
Ye see that he has taen the rue,
But gif he's gane, I've gotten you."
"But then,"quo he,"I'm no sae sonsie
To haud away the wights unchancie;
For fient a fay durst e'er appear
Sae lang as he was gaun you near.
Yet, rather than ye gang your lane,
I'll do my best to see ye hame.
But, bless me, Betty, gies your han,
Ye look as ye could hardly stan;
There's surely something wrang or ither,
Ye ne'er let ae sab wait anither."
Kindly her han and arm she gaed:
Awa they slipt but naething said.
Yet, in that silent situation,
For what would he hae changed his station?
Right fain would she hae tell't him a,
Yet something aye within said na.
The heart was fu, 'twould fain been out,
But couldna light on words to suit,
Till memory stept across the min,
And waked the days o auld lang syne.
The hawthorn yet stood on the brae
That shielt them mony a simmer day;
Whar the slee pyat wont to hap,
The lanely cushat cooin sat.

Their seats and houses reared wi care,
The stanes lay scattered here and there;
And saugh trees, planted by his han,
Waved high their taps, and hid the stran.
What various thoughts the mind pourtrayed, -
His cheek to hers he saftly laid,
While sympathy, wi simple haud,
Forgot that modesty forbad.
E'en waefu " Ken," with gratefu ee,
Wad lick her han and whisk her knee,
Till she wad straik and clap his head,
Then joyfu on the way he'd lead.
"O Bess! thir scenes are dear to me,
But doubly sae when blest wi thee;
Dear as when hope the mind employs,
To picture scenes o future joys:
Though simmer has withdrawn his beams,
They're aften present in my dreams,
Wi a the flow'ry birth o May,
When we, like them, were young and gay.
Ilk hill and dale, and buss, and green,
Whispers how happy we hae been.
I fear they'll ne'er return again -
And pleasure past but heightens pain:
As wintry calms in mildest form,
Prove aft the prelude to a storm.
When ye war near I aye was glad,
And seemed to see ye aft when fled:
As music through the ear does thrill,
Though ceased, we seem to hear it still.
I kentna then, as I ken noo,
What ill the want o wealth could do;
Or, if for't e'er my heart did ache,

'Twas only, truly, for thy sake.
Me, fondest fancy whiles would move,
To picture a the joys o love ;
Till I my wishes could explain,
And some day ye would be my ain:
Then a my fears to air wad gang
Now tell me was I right or wrang?"
"It's no for me," quo she, "to say
What may be done some ither day;
Nor can I weel, e'en now define
The thoughts, when young, that crossed my min;
But this I ken, as weel's yoursel,
That some gang daft when they hear tell:
And mair partic'larly my mither,
Whene'er she kens that we're thegither.
On marriage I'm no fully bent,
Nor do I yet ken their intent;
But soon as I can guess their views,
I'll sen ye twa lines o the news.
Ye needna doubt - I'll no forget -
But, see! we're maist come to the yett:
Ye'd better turn." - Quo he, " Ye'll mind,"
So kissed, shook hans, and parted kind;
While back he scoured out owre the bent,
And thought his journey no ill spent.
      The paitrick whirred alang the ley,
The pliver whistled o'er the fey,
The bleater coursed aboon the bog,
Up the glens crap the lazy fog,
The saft win shook the witherin grass;
But Nature, in her hamely dress,
Wi her habiliments laid by,
Can please us, when the hopes are high.

Amang his mountains bleak and bare,
He hugs himsel wi hamely fare,
And sleeps as soun 'tween earthen was
As lords within their lofty has.

Part 5
The Wylie Merchant

But ah! there was a merchant loon,
That lived in the neist borough toun,
A wily, spruce, and nipping blade,
Wha made the penny aye his trade,
And played upon the country foibles,
Or soothed the lasses up wi baubles.
To every creed he tuned his strain,
And sauld his music aye for gain;
Had aft the art, whar'er he went,
To mak fouk wi themsels content:
This gart them aft his fauts forget;
For flattery's aye a sicker bait.
        Wi three half-crowns he wan at hirdin,
He toiled till he had got a birden
O coats, and gowns, and corduroys,
And lace, and gauze, and ither toys;
Nor after that was he mair slack,
But gat a beast to bear his pack.
        At John's he'd stay baith weeks and days,
And clash wi Kate, and sell them claes
And whiles upon the trump would play,
Or sing the dools o "Duncan Gray,"
Or gie to Bet, though she was sma,
A screed o lace to make her braw:
And aften to himsel would hum -

"Thy tocher will do good to some."
A throwgaun, rattlin, merry chiel,
And fouk a thocht him doin weel;
Till a at ance he made a stop,
But after soon set up a shop.
     When Betty chanced to gang to fair
To buy some braws, or sell her ware,
Although the shop was e'er sae prest,
He'd spier for her and a the rest;
Would rub his hans, her chin would pat,
Say, "Love, and dear, and bonny Bet,
Do ye no want a braw new gown,
A muslin mantle, or a crown?
John, show these shawls and sarsnets, quick,
That cam frae Lonon the last week.
Now, I can tell ye, without flatterin,
Baith for the cheapness and the pattern,
They're most astonishin to see;
But look yoursel, and heedna me.
I'll mak them - but ye needna tell,
Nane gets sae low, love, but yoursel."
Then wad he kindly lead her ben,
And seat her in the parlour en,
Whar tea and trockery a war ready,
That weel might sert the brawest lady;
A Roman urn wi siller slabs,
And China ware wi giltet gabs.
     "But sic a change was never seen
Bless me, ye're turned a strappin quean,
Sin I stayed at your faither's house,
He was an honest man, and douce!
And then, sae fluently ye speak,
And sic a blossom's on your cheek;

Though our town nymphs be trig and braw,
Shame fa me but ye ding them a.
I'm sure the lads are rinnin mony
For you, sae rich, and braw, and bonny:
Wha saw your craft about the gloamin,
Wad see them thick and thrang a-roamin."
A this he said. Then she again -
"O, sir, ye're surely makin game
Or think ye I can a believe
What ye in compliment me give?
But, Mr Din, if ane might speir,
Ye've haen a house this mony a year,
Wi a things fit to comfort life -
How live ye thus without a wife?"
"I own," quo he, "in this I'm wrang,
But then the warl held me thrang;
And, ere that I can get gear wi me,
The fient a ane, I fear, will hae me,
Ye see I've near lost mark o mouth,
And lasses aye are fond o youth.
But tell me truly, now, could ye
Be happy wi the like o me?
In this, dear Bet, I am not mockin,
Though whiles I hae a gate o jokin.
O! what a pleasure I wad hae,
To keep you like a lady gay." -
But here the prentice in did pop,
And o the dialogue made a stop.
So she gaed hame while it was light,
And dreamt o ribbons a the night.
For fashion's freaks sae filled her head,
She soon forgat her shepherd lad;
Or if she mint him sin that night,

She saw him in a different light -
A decent lad, and gien to readin,
But that has neither house nor haudin;
And then my mither's peace 'twad kill:
Bairns aye should do their parents will -
They maistly aye do weel does that.
Weel, fouk in towns live trig and neat,
And some do say, if poortith come,
That love, like reek, flies up the lum.
Thus by the dint o soundest reason,
She found her former passion treason -
Let doatin fools say what they will,
A woman will be woman still.

      But in the morning when she raise,
She showed them a her braw new claes,
And tauld auld Kate she never saw
The merchant hae a shop sae braw.
"Frae Lonon now his goods he brings:
I'm sure he sells a unco things.
The factor's wife, wi young Miss Grace,
Were there and bought a new pelisse,
A trimmed wi gimp o velvet green,
The prettiest thing that e'er was seen.
The fouk say, a the country roun,
He sells the cheapest in the town
And then, he's aye sae frank and free:
Yestreen he gart me stay to tea,
And showed me a before we stentit,
Out through the house - it's newly pentit;
And meikle mair than I can name,
O furniture that's new come hame;
Syne tret me to a glass o gin,
And wondered that ye ne'er cam in."

"Guid sooth," quo Kate, "lass, I'll be bun
To lay a plack, forgain a pun,
He's on you thrown a wily ee:
For weel I mind when ye were wee,
He'd please you aft when I was thrang,
And sing you mony a merry sang,
And bring you fairins frae the fair,
And speak about your bonny hair.
Although the town's fouk wi their havers,
About him raise sic lies and clavers,
The fient a civiler chiel there's in't:
Fouk aye should roose the ford's they fin't."
　　　To please auld John, too, he had skill,
Wi routh o cracks and routh o yill,
"How the last Parliament that sat
Was busied wi the Lord knows what,
O' kirk and state and dark petitions,
And souderin mighty coalitions;
What Wellington had done in Spain;
How foreign war keeps up the grain:
That tax and tithes were now nae play,
And land was risin every day:
How the rude Russians frae the woods,
Had soused poor Boney in the suds,
And cowed his garments by his wame,
And shaved his beard, and sent him hame,
And raised a dearth 'mang Paris barbers;
How Britain shored to block his harbours:
But some said when it cam a thow,
They feared again his beard wad grow,
And learn the Cossacks a new fling,
And cow their whiskers 'gain the spring.
How Yankee's sons, wi wicked speed,

Wi Madison at their board head,
Had led our brigs and boats a dance,
And taen their trade awa to France.
How, gif the Papist Bill would pass,
'Twould bring the nation to distress
Sound orthodox it would enthral,
And fill their seats wi sons o Baal
For Satan and the Man o Sin
Need nought but their wee finger in,
And Gibeon's sons wi a their clatter,
Should hew the wood and draw the water" -
Auld John gaes hame, and thought and said,
"Weel, yon chiel has an unco head."
   So a bowls now rowed square and right,
The auld fouks saw their prospect bright.
While Betty's heart was blythe and gay,
The merchant cam ae King's fast-day:
They a a kindly welcome gae'm,
And treat him weel wi curds and cream;
When in return fu kind was he,
And fetched auld Kate a pun o tea.
They cracked owre a the news in town,
And preed a drap to synd them down;
Syne tauld his erran pat and plain,
And saw it wasna that ill taen.
Betty looked down and held her tongue;
Her mither doubted she was young,
And aiblins whiles might act amiss,
In managin a house like his.
"Indeed," quo John, "I canna tell,
I wished her aye to please hersel
And whar she liket best to gang,
Unless 'twere a the farer wrang;

It's nae faut they that bear the load
Should hae the choosin o the road,
And they wha climb the slippery tree,
Should pluck the fruits that please the ee.
The great respect to her ye've paid,
Should surely aye be duly weighed:
What say ye, dochter, speak out plain
Your answer to the gentleman?"
She tarried lang, as in a swither,
Then sought a fortnight to consider
While he, contentit, slippet hame,
For, 'las! his fire edge was gane.

Part 6
The Luckless Errant

But by some how it soon cam out,
And neibours talked o't roun about,
And through the countra flew ding dang,
That thae twa wad be wed ere lang;
When some, nae doubt, through frienly views,
Tauld Sandy the unwelcome news,
Whilk sic a stoun sent to his breast
As some hae foun but few exprest.
      Hae no seen the towering pine
Spread out its arms to western wind,
Or bathe its bud in April dews,
While wild birds warbled through its boughs,
Till loud the northern blasts are borne,
Its foliage thinned, its branches torn?
Or hae ye seen the parent mild,
Bow o'er his sickly only child,
While silent griefs his bosom wound,

Unmindful of his friends around?
    So stood he, like a statue dumb,
While croudin thoughts his mind o'ercome;
Or, if a gleam stept cross his mind,
O days when she was true and kind,
Then wicked memory, ne'er asleep,
That brings the sour as weel's the sweet,
Brought to his mind anither matter -
How she had never sent the letter;
Or when he saw her e'er sinsyne,
To be their lanes did ne'er incline.
    Now what though simmer roun did bloom,
And breezes bore the saft perfume;
The birken bank or blushing flower
To please him now had lost their power;
The bird that charmed him in the spring,
Was now an idle chitterin thing;
The burnie singin owre the linn
But stunned and deaved him wi its din:
His mind, retiring, shunned ilk joy,
Like sickly virgin, pale and coy:
Even a the pleasures life could gie,
He viewed them wi a jaundiced ee.
    To ease his mind frae doubts and dread,
And see gif a was true was said,
At midnight hour, wi grief opprest,
When thoughtless sauls were at their rest,
He stalked awa through win and rain,
And sought her door wi meikle pain,
There at the window peepit in,
But a was still and dark within
His bane, his bliss, his a was there;
His hopes were dull, his heart was sair;

Each wonted signal now he tries,
He chaps, he whispers, hoasts, and cries,
"Oh I are ye sleepin, Betty dear?"
Yet she lay still and doughtna hear;
But the unchancie curs within
Soon heard, and made a gowlin din:
Till Kate waked, wi an unco fike,
Cries "What's ado! the dogs gane gyte!
The Lord look till us and our wean,
For something surely cad her name;
Like a wild skreich borne on the wind,
And thrice it duntit on the grund:
Wi sic a soun my lugs were stouned
The night afore Jean Tamson drowned -
John, did ye hear that voice sae deep?"
"Hout, I heard nought - lie still and sleep."
    His proud heart dunted back wi grief,
To be thus cow'ring, like a thief,
A chilled wi cauld, and wet wi rain,
For ane that felt nae for his pain.
His patience could nae langer thole;
He stapt twa lines through the key-hole.
    The east win blew, wi haustanes keen;
The lightning gleamed the blasts between:
His road lay owre a dreary moor,
And by a castle's haunted tower,
Whar howlets screamed wi eerie din,
Till vaults re-echoed a within.
The spate spewed owre ilk burn and sleugh,
The tod screamt eldricht frae the cleugh,
Auld Dee spread wide his darkened waves,
And roared amang his rocky caves;
The moon and stars their light withdrew,

And hid their heads frae human view,
As daunderin slow, he stalked his lane,
A wearied, wan, and wae-begane,
His fondest fairy dreams were fled -
He sighed, and wished him wi the dead.
    O! thou dread, wily, wicked pest,
That laughs at poverty distrest,
Wham sighs and sorrows seldom move,
Art thou the gentle power of Love?
Mild is thy visage, gay and young,
Thy voice like fabled syren's song;
Soft is thy dalliance for an hour,
Ere yet equipt with all thy power:
But where with sceptred power thou reigns,
Thou bindst thy subjects up in chains, -
Chains stronger far than bands o brass,
Then leaves them, raving in distress.
    But when the ruddy streaks o dawn
Had spread their light owre loch and lawn,
Up sprang the lark, on early wing,
And waked his field-mates round to sing;
When Kate, aye eident for their weal,
Gat up, and maist fell owre the wheel;
Her brats she on her bouk was drawin,
Afore the cock had ceased frae crawin;
Then to the hallan graips her way,
And looks the lift, to judge the day.
    But, Sandy, ye were waur than mad,
To shoot your sonnets sic a road:
For, coming near the water-kit,
She sees some white thing at her fit,
As back she owre the threshold treadit -
But, praise be blest! - she couldna read it.

First thought it was a Johnnie Napier,
Then deemed it Betty's curling paper;
Flang't in the bole behint the lum,
Rakes down the coals, and lights her gun.
But breakfast done, and reading by,
The men to hill, and Kate to kye,
When Betty, busied at her wheel,
And lilting owre Lord Moira's reel,
Hard by the bole had taen her stan,
She sees the scrawl, and kens the han.
The paper trembled as she read,
And aye her colour came and gaed: -
"Thou fause, though fairest o thy kind,
That wounds my peace, and racks my mind,
Canst thou thy Sandy's heart disdain,
And slight his love for sordid gain;
That ance his fondest hopes would cheer,
And bless him with thy presence dear?
I fain wad seen thee by thysel,
To tak the lang and last farewell,
Afore that waefu knot be tied,
That bins thee for anither's bride,
And leads thee, blushing in thy charms,
Into a happy rival's arms.
Far be't frae me, that I dissuade,
Or blame you for the choice you've made:
But had ye been content to gie
Your han through life, and luck wi me,
For you ilk care and cross I'd meet,
And toiled through winter's win and weet:
Nor should it e'er been wardly gain,
I think, should cost you grief or pain.
But Fate sic favours doughtna deign;

Alas! ye never can be mine.
Adieu! and may ye happy be,
As e'er I thought to've been wi thee."
     She wi amazement on't did stare,
And wondered how it·could come there;
Stunned and confused her senses seem,
Like ane new wakened frae a dream.

Part 7
The Beggar Bodie

But soon cam in, and stapt her study,
A silly, faichless, beggar bodie.
The tattered remnants o her claes
Looked like remains o better days:
Though young in years, seemed auld in grief,
And faintly sought some sma relief.
Within her withered, wearied arm,
There lay a silly, thrawart bairn,
Wi cauld and hunger black and blue,
That seemed to swap some face she knew.
The waefu thing began to greet;
She bade her come and warm its feet;
Then sighed and pitied sair her lot,
And gae her kail, warm frae the pot.
Then in cam Kate and did her ee,
Says, "Honest woman, where live ye?
Hae ye a man; or is he dead,
That ye've sae early tried the trade?"
The waefu body hung her head.
"Indeed, gudewife, I've neist to nane,
Although I chanced to hae this wean.
Some's born to poortith, some to plenty;

Some ne'er do weel, though e'er so tentie.
My fouks a died when I was wee,
And now I'm come to what ye see
And a by a fause merchant loon,
Lives het and fou within the town.
He has brought me to meikle shame,
And hurt my peace, my health, and name.
Quo Kate, "Can that be Mister Din?"
"Indeed," quo she, "the vera ane.
My gutcher, too, now he's awa,
That lived within the Rattan Raw -
Ye aiblins kent him - Andro Reid -
He seldom saw the faut I did.
Sae I got plenty o my will; -
We lived by selling hame-brewed yill.
Rab aft cam owre at gloamin's e'e,
To tak a drap, and crack wi me.
He soon turned mair than common kind;
But I could never bow my mind,
Though he would vow and praise my face,
Till ance the priest had said the grace.
But by his devilish Judas skill
He soon brought a things to his will:
He said he had some secret ens,
Forbye the angerin o his friens;
But for to show that he was kind,
And put a doubts out o my mind,
He kent a priest that lived near by,
Wha soon our hans and hearts would tie;
But I should stay at hame as yet,
Till ance we saw a time mair fit.
Alas! I sawna where I ran,
Like ithers, fond to get a man:

Owre deep for me the scheme was laid,
I deemed it gospel a he said;
For what we wish we soon believe,
Which gars me now baith greet and grieve.
The priest turned out - what need I tell,
A maskëd villain like himsel.
I o him now began to doubt,
For he cam seldomer about;
And when I rued, and vowed, and grat,
He soothed me on wi this and that.
We carried on a time o sinnin,
(For evil needs but a beginnin,)
Till, by our frequent being thegither,
I fand I soon would be a mither,
Sae when it could nae mair be hid,
'Twas then I o my spark got rid;
He shunned me now where'er we met,
And scarce a word I e'er could get:
Then when I gaed to speak to him,
He aye was thrang, or no within.
So now my gutcher I maun tell,
When I could hardly gang mysel,
His time-worn cheek yet paler grew,
The dim red frae his faen lip flew;
'Oh! luckless bairn - this for my care!'
He saw my tears, and said nae mair,
But took his staff, and awa he set,
But an unholy welcome gat.
Rab would do nought but curse and swear,
And ca me names I ill could bear;
Denied our marriage, time and place,
And said he hardly kent my face,
And would advise us, as a friend,

To gang to some I better kend,
For gif we gae him mair abuse,
He'd tak us to a bigger house.
We tried the law - the law was vain,
It only brought expense and pain;
He took it to a higher court;
We hadna siller to gie for't;
A poind was ca'd, we maun remove,
For saying things we couldna prove.
Feeble, in want and sair disgrace,
We wistna where to show our face.
My gutcher cheered me, said his prayers
But grief brought down his auld grey hairs,
And ere this wee thing saw the light,
His een were closed in endless night,
And left us, at its luckless birth,
Twa waefu outcasts on the yirth."

      Nae mair she said, wi grief opprest,
But sighs and sabs made out the rest.
The bairnie looked wi piteous ee,
And screeched, and wailed, and clasped her knee.
So feeble ivy round doth clim'
Yon leafless tree hangs o'er the linn.

      "His presence bless us a!" quo Kate,
"The creature's in an unco state;
If a be true that she has said,
He's a debauched and devilish blade."
While Betty's wheel ceased to gang roun,
She jimply scapit frae a swoon:
Her rock turned yellow, green, and blue;
She fand hersel she kentna how;
And cried out loud, "I winna hae him!"
Quo Kate, "The Lord defend us frae him!

Or ony ane o sic like kind
Should e'er be boun to me or mine."
        So John was tauld o a that passed,
And a took out a full protest.

Part 8
The Conclusion

But the neist week they lost a quey,
Whilk strayed awa to Sandy's fey;
Young Betty blythely gaed to get her,
And he, as joyfu saw and met her.
He spak, she smiled, and looked fu sweet
Twa hearts were ne'er so fond to meet.
He clasped her in his arms, and than
He was a truly happy man.
But wha, think ye, could tell the pow'r
O love within that happy hour?
Or how he pressed, and she was kind -
Let lovers picture't in their mind,
That feel the favour o sic blisses,
Though naething passed but harmless kisses.
        Thus hae I seen, in flowery spring,
The rose-tree forth her blossoms fling;
Spread her saft fragrance through the air,
Near by the lily, blooming fair,
Though rudely bent wi showery blast,
Look fairer when the storm was past.
        She vowed, o gear her friens sae proud,
Might seek out for her wha they would,
Be't priest, or laird, or limb o law,
Shed wed wi him afore them a;
Then bade him come some day and see

What way the auld fouk would tak wi;
And meikle mair they spak about,
For lovers' talk runs seldom out.
When blinks o day were partly gane,
They parted blythe, to meet again.
　　　But proud o heart, and damp wi fear,
To face auld Kate, for want o gear:
'Twas thus he stack, 'tween hope and doubt,
Till time a difference brought about.
Fortune for ance brak through her rules,
Grown weary aye o favourin fools,
And blest him wi a lump o siller,
Though he had ne'er made courtship till her.
　　　He had an uncle, without weans,
Lived lang amang the sugar canes.
Had sauld his soul by unfair means,
To win a fortune to his friens;
Sae destitute o ought was gude,
For gowd would sauld his flesh and blude;
Had gruesome caudrons ever boiling,
And scores o slaves around him toiling;
And aften would himsel solace
Within their greasy black embrace.
It's a in taste; but as they tell,
He aye was whipper-in himsel;
And gart the lash wi rigour crack,
Till red sweat started frae their back;
It cured his spleen to hear their squeels,
To score their hips, and clog their heels:
'Twas strange that hell he never feart,
For nought on yirth comes half sae near't;
But death strak in and scorched his liver,
And boiled his brains up in a fever;

So he maun die, and leave them a
To far-aff friens he never saw.
      Now Sandy was nae langer blate,
But cam to visit John and Kate,
While Bess was unco blythe to see him;
And a a hearty welcome gie him;
Kindly for a his kin they speir;
Says, "ye're an unco stranger here";
Sae soon an ingle was brought ben,
And soon they plucked the hoodet hen;
A claith was spread upon the board,
And Sandy's Mistered every word.
Kate wi her ain han set a chair;
John said a grace like ony prayer;
Then heaps his plate wi beef and kail,
And bids him tak a hearty meal;
Syne round they swill the barley broo. -
      O wealth! what is't ye canna do?
Thou get'st us friends, baith kind and mony;
Maks hamely lasses dear and bonny;
Opes the blate wooer's steekit mouth
And gars the lawyer speak the truth:
Maks wee men great men, mony a time
Gars poets preach, and pipers rhyme;
And clears up mony a point o faith:
In short, reverses a but death.
      Thus luck and love did baith combine
Wi youth their hearts and hans to join
His proffers now were frank and warm,
Nor did they deem his offers harm.
The Haly Chanter gat a crown;
A cart was yokit for the town,
To buy the braws they aff did bicker,
Forbye a lade o laeves and liquor;

Then at the manse, as they cam by,
Bespake Mess John, the knot to tie.
Thus time, as usual, glade away;
But Sandy thought ilk hour a day,
Till ance that happy e'en drew near
To fill his arms wi a was dear;
He thanked his stars and happy fate,
That blest him wi his bonnie Bet.
     It's no for my weak muse's wing
The joys o bridal nights to sing,
Nor paint the scenes o virtuous love,
Where twa fond hearts in union move.
Yet, though she downa weel express't,
There's some, nae doubt, will try to guess't. -
Nor will I tak in han to say
They were quite happy monie a day,
And aye were full as fond o ither
As the first day they gaed thegither.
There's nane exempt frae life's cares,
And few frae some domestic jars;
A whiles are in, and whiles are out,
For grief and joy come time about.
And they that doubt may try, and see
Whether it's them that's right, or me.
But, if content stays here ava,
Ye'd think their chance was no that sma.
     Now, should some critic snap and snarl
At this lang tale, without a moral;
Say, I've intruded on his time,
Wi lengthened play o doggerel rhyme,
I freely own, 'twas wrote for pleasin -
This age is not for moralizin:
For this is law, says Vicar Bray,
To suit yoursel to present day.

Culloden
Tune *"Oh! are ye sleepin, Maggie?"*

The heath-cock crawed o'er muir and dale,
    Red raise the sun, the sky was cloudy,
While mustering far, wi distant yell,
    The northern bands marched stern and steady.

Chorus - Oh! Duncan, Donald's ready!
        Oh! Duncan, Donald's ready!
        Wi sword and targe he seeks the charge,
        And frae his shouther flings the plaidie.

Nae mair we chase the fleet-foot roe,
    O'er down and dale, o'er mountain flyin;
But rush like tempests on the foe,
    Through mingled groans the war note cryin.

        Oh! Duncan, Donald's ready, &c.

A prince is come to claim his ain,
    A stem o Stewart, frienless Charlie;
What Highlan han its blade would hain,
    What Highlan heart behint would tarry?

        Oh! Duncan, Donald's ready, &c.

I see our hardy clans appear,
    The sun back frae their blades is beamin;
The Southern trump falls on my ear,
    Their bannered lions proudly streamin.

        Now, Donald, Duncan's ready!
        Now, Donald, Duncan's ready!
        Within his hand he grasps his brand;
        Fierce is the fray, the field is bluidy.

But lang shall Scotlan rue the day
    She saw her flag sae fiercely flyin;
Culloden's hills were hills o wae;
    Her honour lost, her warriors dyin.

        Duncan now nae mair is ready!
        Duncan now nae mair is ready!
        The brand is fan frae out his hand,
        His bonnet blue lies stained and bluidy!

Fair Flora's gane her love to seek;
    Lang may she wait for his returnin;
The midnight dews fa on her cheek;
    What han shall dry her tears o mournin?

        Duncan now nae mair is ready, &c.

Dark Rolling Dee
Tune *"Banks of the Devon"*

Dark rolling Dee, with thy heath-covered mountains,
Thy wild rugged rocks by yon black birken glen,
That claim'st thy supplies from the cold mossy fountains,
And minglest thy treasures with low-spreading Ken:

Scenes of my youth, where my wishes oft wander,
Where the traces of nature my bosom first warmed;
For low on thy banks, where thy waves sweet meander,
Spreads the low blushing rose that my fancy has charm'd.

How fain would I woo thee, sweet flower, to my bosom,
And sever thy stalk from its first native stole,
Where the kind breath of love should invite thee to blossom,
Though the chill blasts of winter around us should howl.

Beauty might fade in the days of December,
But the noon-tide of friendship around us should beam;
The fervour of youth I would fondly remember,
And shield thy sweet blossoms by Dee's winding stream.

On the Death of The Rev. Dr. Murray, Late Professor of Oriental Languages in the University of Edinburgh

Mourn, Gallovidia, o'er thy heathy bed!
Thy favourite child, in the cold earth is laid:
Thy far-famed son, so skilled in learn'd lore,
Shall teach our minds or mend our hearts no more!
Oft hast he pored through learning's lonely way,
Amidst thy rocks and pathless mountains grey;
Friendless, unknown, by adverse fortune driven,
With scarce an aid but this - the light of Heaven!
'Twas his the depths of Language to unlock,
What every tongue in every clime hath spoke:
A key, the sacred oracles to show,
And angels' tongues to teach to men below. -
Far shone the light, and thawed the stony heart;
The nations saw, and wondering, owned his art.
        Thus, with the Prophet, in a dry parched land,
The obedient streams rushed forth at his command:
Far flowed the waters through the desert wide; -
Israel believed, and nations blest their guide.
Full well he knew to weigh the wondrous whole
Of shining orbs, that on their axles roll -
To trace their circles through a pathless road,
Till the proud Atheist, trembling, owned a God.
Alike this world its various parts to scan,
What laws best polish, and what shackle man;
Of every tie that binds the human heart -
The laws of morals, and each noble art;
To wake the numbers of the Muse's lay,
Or deep-toned grief, or sportive satire gay.
In him each gentler passion did contend -

The tender Husband and the faithful Friend.
Though lofty Science kindly on him smiled,
Yet modest manners marked him for her child.
Long hast thou, Cree, swept through thy lakes and woods,
And with the ocean mixt thy crystal floods;
But long thy swains shall mark the varied year,
Ere such a shepherd on thy banks appear.
And as the rocks shall be his lasting fame;
MURRAY shall live while Scotland boasts a name.
      To thee, the mourner, and the Mother fair,
That's lonely left to all a widow's care,
On his Loved Pledges let thy kindness flow,
Till Hope shall triumph o'er remembered woe. -
Be thine the task to guide their helpless youth,
In all the paths of innocence and truth,
Till classic learning dawn across the mind,
And riper Reason every sense refine:-
Like him, to claim their country's best regard,
Are the fond wishes of a simple Bard.

The Disappointment

To thee, that ilk wish in my bosom can claim,
Wha aften I think on, but seldom I name,
I send these few lines, wi a hearty good will -
Though in writing love verses I sair doubt my skill:
Yet though the coy muse a drear silence should keep,
The wrongs that I bear, and affection, shall speak.

What stopt ye yestreen that ye cam na to see
Your lover sae lonely that doats upon thee?
The winds were a laid, and the evenin was clear;
How sweet was the silence! but ye cam na near!
That hour was a time that reflection might suit:
The leaves they lay still, and the birdies were mute;
The gowan was sippin the saft siller dew;
The brown heather waved, wi its bells red and blue;
The moon shewed the sheet o the clear mountain stream,
That moved the lake's bosom to dance to her beam.

But I flew to the spot where the trystin was set,
To the auld scrogged hawthorn, where aft we had met.
My hopes they were high, but my heart was soon sair -
A hare happit by me - but ye were na there!

I looked and I listened, I hummed o'er a sang;
The south it grew gloomy, the time it grew lang;
I saw the dim shade o the cloud passin by;
The stars seemed disordered, and shot in the sky;
Loud roared the blast dreary, and bended the woods;
The moon she seemed feared, and veiled her in clouds.
Tall trees, lately viein in stature and form,
Flung round their arms widly, and raved in the storm:
The winds and the waves seemed wi nature at war -
But my mind was as restless, and gloomier far.

The statesman may storm when his schemes hae been crost,
The merchant may grieve when his prospects are lost;

But neither can equal the keen throbbin smart
Of hope disappointed, that wounds the fond heart:
'Tis mine all to feel, as in silence I moan,
Whilst thou, like a careless spectator, look'st on.
 What though I be friendless, and poorer than you,
My life's nae less leal, and my love nae less true;
Though friends should deny that you e'er should be mine,
Might na we whiles meet yet to talk o langsyne:
To tell the first spot where our fancy was moved;
How fair was your beauty, how dearly I loved?
With arms clasped around you, my joys would o'erflow,
When hid frae this world, and a its vain show.
How sweet the dark blasts frae your bosom to shroud!
Love lives in retirement, but dies in the crowd.
 Though calm-bluided Prudence her sons may direct
To walk wi decorum, each step circumspect;
They ne'er knew Love's passions, its beams, or its storms,
That ill can be guided by rules or by forms.
The daisy blooms sweet in its own native plain,
Though chilled by the cauld blast, and beat by the rain:
But see, in the garden, how short is its day;
It withers in riches, its blossoms decay!
 Perhaps ane mair wealthy your bosom has charmed,
The glare o whose gold your young fancy has warmed,
And I left alane here to languish in pain,
While every new day adds a link to the chain.
 But where do I wander? - I meant but to tell
The simple auld story, - I love you still well;
And when that the sun is far fled to the west,
When lambs frae their gambols are gane to their rest,
Shall I hope then to see you, to bless these lone arms,
While the moon's silent beams shall add grace to your   charms?
Oh! haste then, my love, to the ance valued spot!
The present be ours, and the past be forgot.

On the Distant View of a Friend's House, in December

How changed is the aspect of yonder retreat,
  Since lately I passed by its bowers!
When Summer shone forth, in his full fervid heat;
Now, the keen biting blasts of the winter winds beat,
  All fledged with the chill snowy showers.

The fair flowing stream, as its course it pursues,
  Is arrested and chilled into stone;
And where are the flowerets that bloomed on its brows -
Its violets, and snowdrops, of delicate hues?
  Alas! they are withered and gone.

How dull the dumb cattle, all cringing with cold,
  As they gaze at the snow-covered heath!
And the poor helpless flocks that are forced from their fold,
The gathering wreath in its bosom has rolled,
  And deprived half their number of breath.

So chilled are my prospects, o'ercast with despair;
  So fate doth my fancy arrest;
With sorrow, and sickness, and canker-toothed care,
My tenderest ties are all vanished to air,
  And chilled the fond hopes of the breast.

The dark sheety clouds, as they're floating on high,
  Their wings o'er the concave extend;
O'er the snow-toppëd mountains in order pass by,
Through their chinks peeps the sun, from a dull murky sky,
  Like the far distant glance of a friend.

As the Sun is the soul of this planet below,
　　To creation new life doth impart;
So friendship beams forth on the wretch worn with woe,
Dispels every doubt, and each fear doth forego,
　　Beams a new love of life on the heart.

Dear Friendship, sweet solace! thy joys let me prove!
　　Thou soother of sorrow and strife -
Thou dearer than riches, thou surer than love -
Thou pledge of each joy that awaits us above -
　　Thou charmer and pilot through life.

Serene is thy aspect, and modest thy mien,
　　Content ever bears up thy train;
And sweet smiling Peace, with her olive so green,
And gay rosy Mirth by thy side may be seen;
　　And Truth ever blesses thy reign.

I've seen thy sweet smiles in yon straw-covered cot,
　　Ere the winter blast thus on it beat;
Thou deign'st oft to visit the cottager's lot,
And cheer the lone haunts of his chequerëd spot,
　　But fly'st from the halls of the great.

Thou smooth'st the dull brow of the dark clouded mind,
　　And sooth'st every pang that is past:
Though crosses may wreck us, or poverty pine,
With thee even the wretched a comfort can find;
　　When absent, the world is a waste.

Donald's Grave
Scene, near Glencoe
Tune "*Yellow Haired Laddie*"

Within the dark bosom of yon lonely glen,
There sleeps my young Donald, the flower of his clan,
In death's silent slumbers, where lowly he's laid
The green sod his target, the cold clay his plaid.

How still lies the heart that to me aye beat true;
And dim now that eye, once a love-speaking blue;
Now withered those soft lips - the roses are flown,
And clotted those locks of a dark bushy brown.

Last night, when the stars from yon dun sky had fled,
And my red stiffened eyes had no more tears to shed,
While the blast thro the broad oak did howl round my head,
Like the bursting of sorrow, or songs for the dead;

When weary with watching, methought he drew near,
And half of his fair form through blood did appear:
Though pale was his aspect, his manner was meek,
And his locked hollow jaw seemed to open and speak: -

"Why mourns my dear Flora along the lone heath?
Can the warm tears of sorrow retrieve me from death?
But the tie's ever binding, although we must part,
And love shall find room still within this cold heart.

"How soft rests the hero who dies for the cause
Of honour and freedom, his country and laws:
The bard's bursting song his achievements shall save,
And chieftains shall sigh as they stalk by his grave.

"We feared not their numbers, that darkened the plain:
They proffered us friendship - their offers were taen;
But the cold-blooded monsters no ties could engage -
In slumbers they slew whom they feared to enrage.

"But the miscreant minion of treacherous power,
His fame and false glory shall fall in an hour:
No sweet-sounding requiem his spirit may claim,
And forgetfulness leave but the dregs of a name.

"Then cease thee, my Flora, oh! cease thee to weep;
My light passing spirit thou marrest of sleep:
Thrice three months are passed since thou should'st been my bride,
But soon shalt thou stretch thee along by my side."

But lo! I awoke, and the lark was on high;
The sun his gold tresses had spread o'er the sky;
Yet still the dark vision this truth did recall,
That the lovely soon fade, and the mighty must fall.

The Fairy Dance

'Twas one even all alone, as the fold I lay tending,
When silence pervaded, and nature was still,
Save the night-raven's whirr where the broad oak was bending,
Or the voice of the fox, as he howled on the hill.
Beneath the grey hawthorn each care was confounded,
Where fancy presented the whimsical trance,
Of hundreds of elves that me quickly surrounded,
As they skimm'd o'er the moorlands to join the fairy dance.

Small was their form, and their motion was lightly,
Their beavers were white, and their vestments were green;
On their front rode a nymph, on a pied steed, so sightly,
Whose rod and deportment betokened their Queen.
Loose flowed her robes, as they shone like the pole-streams
That shake o'er the sky with a quivering glance;
And bright shone her face like the silvery moon's mild beams,
While thus she addressed them, to join the fairy dance:

"Come, ye fleet elves, and ye spirits of ether,
Now is the time that our revels we keep,
Brushing the dew from the low-bending heather,
While the dull sons of earth lie involvèd in sleep.
Minstrels now meet, let your music be sounding;
Partners be clasping - in couples advance;
Hence with dull care; let your joys be abounding;
Trip to the moon-beam the gay fairy dance."

Shrill sounds the pipe, still the low glens repeating,
Meet, joined the harp, with its melody low;
Now airy they wheel, and now lovingly meeting,
As gaily they flit on the light skiffing toe.
High beat me heart - how my fancy was cheered;
Mehtought that to meet them I forth did advance;
But the melody ceased, and the scene disappeared -
So fleeting our joy, like the gay fairy dance!

On Fickleness

Say, what a captious creature's man,
        That's never near contented?
Let fortune favour a she can,
        Yet still there's something wanted.
Whate'er we hae we soon despise,
        Be't lasses, lair, or money;
While what we want we highly prize,
        And think it gude and bonny -
                While unpossessed.

The beggar, free frae tax and charge,
        Sighs for a house and haddin;
The cotter wants his yard made large,
        An's o a mailin bodin.
There's jobber John, the donsie man,
        Whas daughter's nearly ready,
Thinks by her shine o pauky een,
        She'll catch some landed body,
                Or priest some day.

The farmer ees the stately ha,
        Forgets his stocks and barns;
The lairdy langs for titles braw,
        For ribbons and for starns:
The Knight a seat - the Lord his Grace;
        The Duke envies the crown;
The king the happy Shepherd's place -
        And thus the wish gaes roun,
                Frae side to side.

See Sawney, in his youthfu days,
    When first he sighed for Sarah;
He walks, he gaunts, he groans, he prays,
    He pines wi love and sorrow;
When harvest days turned dreigh and warm,
    'Twas then they first fell gracious;
He mawed her rig wi manfu arm,
    Till like a brose his face was,
        Wi sweat that day.

To pick the prickles frae her han
    To him now's near Elysium;
To plait her locks, or bear her can,
    Can never fail to please him;
She was nane o the scornfu pack,
    Aye bent on feuds or fleein;
But stopt ae night, and took a crack,
    And saved the lad frae deein
        An unco death.

For her he shook the hasky strae,
    And kaved the corn fu neatly,
And bore her beuk ilk Sabbath day,
    To keep her sma and featly.
O'er every stran he took her han,
    And prest it kin and slily;
Bore streekit claith aboon her face,
    Although the day was drily,
        To shield her form.

But wha can stop the wind to blaw,
 Or keep the cock frae crawin,
Or haud ghaists frae the haunted ha,
 Or me frae sleep at dawin?
Or, wha can tether tide or time,
 Or bind the frail affections;
Or stay the weakly waverin mind,
 Wi a love's kind connexions,
  And tender ties?

Soon as the boasted trifle's gane,
 That downa thole the namin,
She sighs, and sabs, and greets her lane,
 And rues the rede o gamin.
Now she pursues, and he forhoos -
 The aftercome o't fears her;
And when they meet, nae kisses sweet,
 Or hinnied words to cheer her,
  Like ance a day.

Where's now the rosy red and white,
 The matchless form and gesture;
That breast for which his soul has sighed
 Or eyes that held him faster? -
The dimples, blushes, smiles, and brows,
 Thy outward charms composed;
And ithers, hid frae lovers' views,
 But sweeter when disclosed? -
  So poets sing.

Hope beets the youthfu lover's flame;
    Enjoyment gars us falter;
The object still remains the same -
    'Tis we ourselves do alter.
Let sage Experience point our views, -
    It never can deceive us;
But Fancy, wi her borrowed hues,
    Aft in the lurch will leave us,
        When reason's shunned.

The Ghost of Crazy Jane

Dark and dismal was the evening;
    Hoarse the raven croaked afar;
Drowsy bats flew round in clusters;
    Faintly beamed the evening star.
Round yon mouldering tower the ivy,
    Closely clasped, though faintly seen;
Highly perched, the night-owl screeching,
    Sung the dirge of Crazy Jane.

Hark! the hollow vaults re-murmured!
    Gusty blasts the turret shake:
Towers did totter on their bases;
    Hungry graves did yawning gape:
When lo! a phantom by me glided,
    Slowly shifting o'er the green,
Says, "Fear me not, thou timorous stranger,
    I'm the Ghost of Crazy Jane!

"Nightly from this grave I wander,
　　To my Henry's lonely bed;
Warding off the evil genius,
　　Hovering round his lovely head.
Till that hour when death shall join us,
　　Never more to part again;
When by my side in this lone grave,
　　He'll repose with Crazy Jane!"

Fled was all that rosy colour,
　　Once adorned her lovely cheek;
Those winning smiles, and dimpling graces,
　　Those modest looks so softly sweet.
The lily neck, the heaving bosom,
　　The graceful and majestic mien -
A faded form, and shrouded spectre,
　　Was all remained of Crazy Jane.

Loud the cock sung out the morning,
　　Mild the sun beamed out the day;
Quick she started as affrighted -
　　Says, "Farewell, I must away!"
Swift she fled on wings of morning,
　　Gliding o'er the dewy scene:
But strong imagination painted
　　All the woes of Crazy Jane.

To Happiness

Say, where is thy dwelling, thou daughter of peace?
    More sweet than the sun-gilded flower;
What thousands await for a glimpse of thy face,
Disappointment and keen-pining Envy to chase,
    From the peasant's lone hut to the tower.

False Hope, with her anchor, would point out the path,
    As her various votaries choose,
By the new-fallowed field, or the blue-bellèd heath,
The statesman's parade, or the warrior's wreath,
    Love, science, a friend, or the muse.

But vain are their pursuits, if passion's unreined,
    Or sickly unsoundness be nigh;
Though Virtue's fair telescope lights the dark mind,
Thou fly'st their fond grasp, like the fast-fleeting wind,
    Or the bright-beaming arch of the sky.

Yet oft dost thou visit the young and the gay;
    Too sweet are the moments to last;
And mirth, wine, and music, can chase Care away
For a night; but, alas! she returns with the day; -
    We painful reflect on the past.

How vain, then, for mortals to pant for the prize?
    'Tis the charter to angels that's given:
This life's a short journey - be patient, be wise -
Unhinge ye from earth; let your prospects arise;
    She dwells not on this side of Heaven.

Henry's Lament.

The sky was blue, the wind was still,
    The blackbird whistled from the brake;
The setting sun's departing beams,
    Gleamed o'er the smooth expanded lake:
The clustering trees on distant hills,
    Seemed in its crystal breast to smile;
And fields, in Summer's beauty drest,
    Confest the weary ploughman's toil.

But Henry's heart was prest wi care,
    Though Nature did her charms disclose;
Her mantle, tinged with various hues,
    But served to tantalize his woes.
The soft wave murmured to his sighs,
    Beside yon leafless foggëd tree;
And aye he sighed and said "Alas!
    "Farewell ye bonny banks of Dee!

"A long farewell, ye happy bowers,
    Where Cultivation spreads her wing;
Ye mansions fair and wood-fringed vale,
    Where warbling choirs delight to sing!
'Twas there where first my youthful heart
    The hopes and fears of love essayed;
There first I saw the opening charms
    Of thee, Maria, peerless maid.

"Her looks were like the summer morn,
    When early sunbeams gild the flower;
Her cheek was like the damask rose,
    While bending with the dewy shower,
But all her beauties to define,
    Would need the noble Raphael's art;
But vain to me his living lines,
    For deep they're graven on my heart.

"'Twas hers to feel, while bended Want,
    Breathed out his woes, his cares, and pain;
Her little all was freely lent;
    He never told his tale in vain.
But if she read the luckless loves,
    Of Anna and Palemon dear,
Anon's magic lines unfold;
    Fast fell the sympathetic tear.

"Oft have I checked the glowing flame,
    That fondly fluttered in my breast,
Lest friends should frown, or fate deny,
    And hurt her wonted peace and rest.
But lovers vain the wish would hide,
    For eyes can eloquently speak;
How soon she answered sigh for sigh,
    While crimson blushes spread her cheek.

"Each look confes't, each touch betrayed,
　　And soft words lingered on my tongue;
And when she spake, upon the tones
　　My ravished ear with transports hung.
Sweet was the task for me to teach,
　　My lovely scholar all my skill;
To touch with art the warbling wire,
　　Or in that hand to guide the quill.

"But fled, alas! are all my joys,
　　While memory rings the heart with pain;
The sweeter joy the keener grief
　　Because it ne'er returns again.
A cruel father's ruthless heart,
　　Forbade us ev'n the last adieu;
And robbed me of my soul's delight -
　　Maria's face no more I view.

"What boots his boasted sacred name,
　　His virtues feigned, all stern and vain;
He bows at Fashion's tinselled shrine,
　　To empty pride and sordid gain.
Ah! gaudy pomp, and gorgeous wealth!
　　For what ye take ye ill repay;
Ye steel the heart for selfish ends,
　　And sweep each social tie away."

The Hills of the Highlands
Tune "*Ewe Bughts, Marion*"

Will ye go to the Highlans, my Mary,
    And visit our haughs and our glens?
There's beauty 'mang hills o the Highlans
    That Lassie i Lowlands ne'er kens.

'Tis true we've few cowslips or roses,
    Nae lilies grow wild on the lea;
But the heather its sweet scent discloses,
    And the daisy's as sweet to the ee.

See yon far heathy hills, where they're risin,
    Whose summits are shaded wi blue;
There the fleet mountain roes they are lyin,
    Or feedin their fawns, love, for you.

They're the scenes o my youth, my dear Mary,
    Where wi solit'ry pleasure I've strayed;
There my forefathers fought in their glory,
    Wi their chieftains they conquered or died.

There the loud roarin floods they are fallin,
    By crags that are furrowed and grey;
To her young there the eagle is callin,
    Or gazin afar for her prey.

The aik, by his ain native fountain,
    His arms out at random hath cast;
And the high towerin fir on the mountain,
    That nods to the sound o the blast.

Or low by the birks on the burnie,
    Where the goat wi her younglins doth rest;
There oft I would lead thee, my Mary,
    Where the blackbird is building her nest.

Right sweet are our scenes i the gloamin,
    When shepherds return frae the hill,
Aroun by the banks o Loch Lomon,
    While bagpipes are soundin sae shrill.

Right sweet is the low setting sun-beam,
    That points owre the quivering stream,
But sweeter the smiles o my Mary,
    And kinder the blinks o her een.

Thy looks would gar simmer seem sweeter,
    And cheer winter's bare dreary gloom;
With thee every joy is completer,
    While true love around us should bloom.

But alas! for my cabin it's lowly,
    And few are my flocks and my kye;
Yet my bosom to thee beats aye truly,
    'Tis what titles or gowd ne'er could buy.

The Southron in a his politeness,
    His airs and his grandeur may shine;
Our hills boast o mair true discreetness,
    And his love is not equal to mine.

Invocation to Spring, 1812

Come, sweet smiling Spring, with thy life-cheering bloom,
    Why so timid and shy to appear?
No dew-droppëd blossoms the morning perfume,
No green glossy garments the forests resume,
    Though time hurries by the short year.

I long for the corn-craik and cuckoo's loud notes,
    To enliven our grey hawthorn bowers;
The lightsome white lambs, as they frisk round the cots,
The seedsman's slow hum as he scatters his oats,
    Thy zephyrs and soft falling showers.

But the dark tyrant, Winter, with thin hoary hair,
    Breathes bleak through the valley and wild:
The half silent songsters forget now to pair,
They wait for thy train, but no vestige is there,
    Save the primrose, thy first lonely child.

Thus mourns sad Britannia, with sorrow and tears,
    For her sons that are dragged to afar;
She waits the nymph Peace; but, lo! what appears!
Whole Europe convulsed, for a series of years,
    With intestine grim bloodshed and war!

So fares't with our prospects in life's early dawn,
    While Hope in gay trappings is drest;
And Love linked with Health, lightly trips o'er the land,
We gaze on the phantom, the curtain is drawn,
    And the bright beams of noon overcast.

Jenny of the Cree
Tune "*Sae dearly's I love Johnny, O*"

Young Jenny blooms the bonniest lass
On a the crystal banks o Cree;
On Gall'way braes wha can surpass
Her dimpl'd cheek or downcast ee?
      There's Susy fair woud me ensnare,
      And blythesome buxom Mennie, O;
      But nane I see sae dear to me,
      Or wins ilk wish like Jenny, O.
      There's Susy fair, etc.

Let wavin woods spread bank an brae,
An heather bells bloom on the hill;
Let lowly flow'rs their blooms display,
She, bonny bud, blooms sweeter still.
      The lav'rock sweet his mate may greet,
      Wi wild-notes blythe an bonny, O;
      But whan she sings he draps his wings,
      An, list'ning, learns frae Jenny, O.
      The lav'rock etc.

What Fortune's gien I'll freely share
Wi my sweet lass o lowly state;
E'en for her sake I'll wish it mair,
To mak her joys the mair complete.
      The sordid wretch may grip and scratch,
      And hoard his soul, the penny, O;
      While in my bower I tent the flower,
      The sweet - the lovely Jenny, O.
      The sordid wretch, etc.

Johnny Gill
A Tale

Kenned ye e'er a social chiel,
    A sober lad, that means nane ill;
But Hymen hooked him in his noose,
    And soured content wi Johnny Gill.

Nane raise mair cheerfu to their wark,
    Peace hovered round his bosom lang;
Wi routh o health his heart was light,
    And blythe he owre the lee-rig sang.

Wha wi him a fur could streekit,
    Or borne a meal sack to his size?
For thrice he banged the miller's man,
    And thrice he won the ploughing prize.

Ruddy was his face, and gracefu,
    When first he hirëd wi Laird Mane,
But ere the winds o ware were blawn,
    Part o's peace and health were gane.

Sally Sloan, baith fair and pauky,
    That made the bed and cleaned the room,
Soon twined him o his manly heart,
    And left poor Johnny's bosom toom.

Gay she spread her curls daily,
    Aye she twinkled wi her een,
Aye she busked her bosom dinkly;
    Whyles a tapered leg was seen.

Soon she saw the lad was dinted,
    Weel it suited wi her plan;
Hadna she her views extended,
    To draw in baith laird and man.

Lang he feart his mind to mint it,
    Sally seemed baith proud and braw;
Sae fierce his love was the first fortnight,
    Fient a wink he slept ava.

Sober was the simmer e'enin,
    Mildly beamed the setting sun,
Glistening on the cottar's window;
    Rowin reek towered frae the lum.

Down a wimplin burnie trotted,
    By a smooth and daisied green;
Here lay sarks, and sheets, and mutches,
    Gowns and ruffles bleaching clean.

On its banks a bower was biggit,
    Theekit owre wi birken leaves;
There gloamin brought the lads and lasses,
    Baith to court and watch the thieves.

Happy bower, that aft has shielded
    Blushes o the bashfu maid;
Though whyles beneath thee hae been happed
    Nymphs that needed nae sic aid.

Here first Fortune favoured Johnny
    To breathe out his lowin flame;
A the lave were soundly sleepin;
    Wha were happier now than them?

Lang they talked o lads and lasses,
    Dresses seen at kirk or fair;
Syne o courting and convoying:
    Lang ere he durst mention mair.

Sally spak o lads bein faithless;
    How it was an awsome sin;
How she seldom saw them happy,
    Matches that hang lang i win.

Johnny joined, and syne drew near her;
    Need I tell what mair they'd say,
Seeing now the ice was broken,
    Hope paved out the after way.

Nae doubt sighs, and vows, and kisses,
    Claps and squeezes o the han,
Thawed through time her snawy bosom;
    Wha can sic a siege withstan?

True it is, they soon were buckled -
    Soon flew by the hinny moon;
But ere sax months slippet slowly,
    Sall brought him a wally son.

Thankless friens by nods and whispers,
    Wi strange fancies filled his head;
Some said he had preed the dainties
    Ere the haly grace was said.

Vexed and crossed, yet kentna weel how;
    Aye he thought his conscience clear:
Sally's mither saw him swithering,
    Whispered saftly in his ear,

That the first was seldom sicker -
    He maun for a truth receiv't;
The laird he spak o learnèd causes;
    But John himsel could scarce believ't.

Ance the carlin kept an alehouse;
    Young anes whyles will kiss the cup;
And daimen wives, when cankers cross them,
    Pree't to keep their courage up.

Sally, gay, and used wi dautin
    By friens or sweethearts a her life,
Now fand but few o nights or days
    Her thoughts had pictured for a wife.

Johnny's glee has now a sameness,
    His hamely fare's no worth a flee;
But weel she loed a tasty neibour,
    Owre a social cup o tea.

He toils, while she maun hae a servant
    To do her drudgery out and in;
Her gentle hans were never made
    To wash his ploughman hose, or spin.

His meal or mart were seldom lastin;
    Kimmers cam and bore't awa;
The beds turned bare and without bosters;
    The milk was suppet, taps and a.

Sall, as bairns turned thick and thicker,
    A her beauties changed their hue;
The laird as nowte grew dear and dearer,
    Turned he wouldna grass the cow.

Meal was dear and scant the kitchen;
    Bairns were sma and ill to rear;
John's locks wore thin but aye he laboured,
    Hoped aye better year to year.

Thus he warsles wi the warld;
    Sally's tongue's baith dreich and fell;
Age and poortith sairly shore him,
    Ere the bairns can fend themsel.

Should ye, lads, a wife that's wanting,
    See some fair lass o'er a gill,
Gif her smirking looks entice you,
    Mind the fate o Johnny Gill.

Beauty seldom proves a blessing;
    The stealing fairy robs the min,
Spreads a lure for knaves and flattery -
    Source o meikle dool and pine.

Hymen's love's baith sweet and lasting,
    If frienly prudence beets the lowe;
But selfish pride, and careless habits,
    Damp the strings o Cupid's bow.

Lines
on seeing a poor old man shunned and
despised at a sacramental occasion

Ah! woefu wreck of wretched man!
Thou, sickening, show'st that life's a span,
    With comforts frail and few;
Thy body, bent by many a year,
Thy feeble limbs reluctant bear;
Thy eye seems wet with blood-stained tear,
    And cheek of clay-cold hue.

On lyart temples, thin and bare,
The zephyr scarce can find a hair,
    To wave a warning round;
But tattered rags he finds enow,
To float and wave, and show to view,
Like autumn's leaves of every hue,
    That, withered, strew the ground.

But see! the thoughtless, proud, and gay,
Poor earthworms! fluttering now in May,
    Fall back and back in rings.
Few heave for thee the pitying sigh;
The Bucks take snuff as thou creep'st by;
The ladies rein the neck and eye,
    And gather in their wings.

Can feeble age you thus affright?
Can poverty thus wound your sight?
    Thus man for man be stunned?
Then ponder well what now ye see;
For who can read the dark decree?
What he is now, ye soon may be,
    And serpent-like thus shunned.

I hear thee heave the heavy moan:
Amidst the crowd thou sigh'st alone,
    And tremblest at the word
Of Gospel peal, that loud is rung
From thundering preacher's pliant tongue,
Unto a giddy lukewarm throng,
    "O Israel, fear the Lord!"

Art thou a sinner, old in crimes,
That in thy youthful, healthful times,
    Oft strayed in folly's road -
Now show'st thy bold presumptuous head
When every youthful passion's dead,
When life's a load - enjoyment fled -
    Thou seek'st the house of God?

Or rather has thy wounded worth
Found nought but cross and care on earth?
    For worth has much to bear. -
Has reckless death thy bosom riven?
Has misery and want thee driven,
Till wrenched of every stay but Heaven?
    Yet hope - nor feed despair:

For HE, whose grace thou fond would'st gain,
HE acts not as the sons of men,
    Nor breaks the bruised reed.
The broken heart to him is dear;
HE soothes, HE wipes the swelling tear;
HE bends from Heaven thy griefs to hear,
    A help and stay in need.

What though the unfeeling crowd aroun,
Within GOD'S house on thee look down,
    For want of rich array?
This borrowed light must soon decline,
When thou in robes of grace may'st shine;
Some future day, perhaps, is thine,
    When theirs is wild dismay.

Lines Written by Wm. Nicholson, The Galloway Poet, on the Right Honourable Thomas James Douglas, Earl of Selkirk's Becoming of Age, 22nd April 1830

The wine cup fill to Selkirk's name
Saint Mary's Isle rejoice -
Around the Dee the trump of fame
Echo each cheering voice.

Though long we all have mourned the loss
Of father kind and dear
Thy worth may prove a source of bless
And dry the widow's tear -

The Peasantry were unemployed
And all things at a stand
But to thee they look quite overjoyed
To find that help's at hand.

The tenant languished in his lease
But who could give him aid?
The dreary times him sore did fleece
And hearts with sorrow bled.

But now our Selkirk's come of age
To take a charge of a
He'll banish all our wants and fears
And drive them far awa.

His manners modest, mild and free
Worthy the race he's come
Long may his tender mither's ee
Live to behold her son.

Oh may he fill his father's chair
His noble line long grace
And may he meet some lovely fair
While honour do his race.

Now Whisky Jean bring forth thy bowl
That long you thought was lost
Her wooden staps frae ilka hole
(*line illegible*)

And drink to Selkirk (*in a*) round
With thee (*illegible*) a
And may we all with joy abound
And care be far awa!

The Lover's Reverie
Tune *"Roslin Castle"*

The mind that's unclouded from sorrow and care,
May relish young spring with the buds of the year,
And Summer yield comfort to those that are free,
Yet they're cheerless and lonely, and lost unto me:
For mine is the empire of sorrow and care,
To be crossed in affection, corroded with fear;
Since my heart's soothing blossom will yield no relief,
But mocks at my cares and despises my grief.

O! Phoebe, thou'rt fairer than love can unfold,
Thou gayest and dearest, e'er nature did mould;
What beams with thy glances to me can compare?
What mien so engaging, or face half so fair?
Does the chain of reflection e'er trace o'er thy mind,
Or point to the moments when once you were kind;
Or can that soft bosom where graces repair
Like the snows of December, be cold and yet fair?

But the titles of honour and dignified birth,
Exalts thee above me, and lessens my worth;
As yon rock which bears diamonds and hangs o'er the sea,
Is gazed at longed for, so thou art to me.
But why need I warble my woes thus alane,
Since Phoebe the fairest deserted the plain? -
Yes I'll sigh with the wild blast, and mourn with the dove,
And I'll soothe me with sorrow for the loss of my love.

A Love Song
Tune "*My jolly young sailor, dear*"

What makes thee thus my hand to press,
    With such an ardent fold;
What makes thee stop and sigh and blush,
    Ere half thy tale be told?
Why do thy eyes, when fix'd on mine,
    Such sweet sensations prove;
Then roll in softness, as they'd weep? -
    It surely must be love.

Why does that wanton hand of thine,
    Thus wander o'er my breast?
The little trembler that's within,
    Thou marrest of its rest.
The silent language of thy sighs,
    Me, too, to sigh doth move;
Yet still you press me to your breast,
    And say "it's all but love." -

Whene'er you lay your cheek to mine
    It makes my pulse to beat;
If lip to lip we e'er entwine,
    You clasp me still more strait,
Till in one breath we seem to live,
    And in one sphere to move;
Such pleasing pain it seems to give,
    It surely must be love.

While thus I lie within your arms -
    O tell an artless maid -
Hast thou on me no base designs,
    Nor sly entrapments laid?
O, no! that heart is full of truth,
    And constant as the dove;
Then I'll resign me to thy arms,
    And trust it's all but love.

Mary's Lament
Tune "*My only jo and deary, O*"

Low, low he lies, without a grave,
    My only hope, my Harry, O,
Entomb'd within yon briny wave,
    Far distant frae his Mary, O!
Trafalgar's shores, where, sadly gay,
Triumphant Victory, in dismay,
Wept o'er her Nelson, cold as clay,
    And my last hopes o Harry, O!

Oft have I o'er the sea-beach stray'd,
    With anxious thoughts, and weary, O;
His dangers made me oft afraid,
    Till soothing Hope would cheer me, O.
While whirling sea-birds round would cry,
With uncouth notes, alang the sky,
Waken my smiling, sleeping boy,
    My only pledge o Harry, O.

Full soon the busy news arriv'd,
    Of victory an' of Harry, O;
Of pleasing comfort it depriv'd
    His luckless, lonely Mary, O!
His gentle spirit's now at rest;
But mine alas! is sore deprest;
No balm shall soothe this troubled breast,
    Till join'd again to Harry, O

To Melancholy

Dull Melancholy! ruefu maid,
Begot in disappointment's shade
By dire Disease, thy donsie dad,
      On Pride, thy mither,
Wi sickly Thought, a pale-faced blade,
      Thy elder brither.

I ken thee by thy ceaseless mane,
Thy staukin gait, and hollow grane,
Thy lantern chafts, and lang cheekbane,
      And deadened ee,
As wanderin through the woods thy lane,
      Thy form I see.

Or saunterin near some auld grey biggin,
Where Time has torn the roof and riggin,
Where ghaists and bogles bead fu trig in,
      Wi midnight croon,
And elves and fairies flisk a jig in,
      To waning moon:

And by thy thoughtfu pensive brow,
Bound roun wi willow, twined wi yew,
And gloomy garb that's dark to view,
      And cypress sash on;
Thou mind'st nae gowns o gaudy hue,
      Nor freaks o fashion;

Nor blushing Spring, wi dews and showers,
Nor Summer gay, wi blowing flowers,
Nor Autumn, though she plenty pours,
    Ye're seldom tentin,
But Winter's wildest, loudest roars
    Ye're maist content in.

What gars ye now be sae prevailin,
And spread your power baith moor and dale on,
Till hamespun fouks in cot and mailin
    Ye blaw your breath on,
And cheerfu Mirth's gay empire's failin
    Wi thoughts distressin?

The great, that o their gear are heedfu,
Though blest wi mair than what is needfu,
By thee are torn wi whim that's dreadfu,
    And discontent,
Till a their joys prove unremeadfu
    For want o want.

O wad ye stay wi foppish loons,
Or prey on priests wi haly gowns,
Or novel nymphs in borough towns,
    Wha ne'er relent ye;
Or fouks wi garters, stars, and crowns,
    Might weel content ye.

Yet aft ye wring the noblest hearts,
When hope her wonted hame deserts,
Or where love shoots his scornfu darts,
    Ye're sure to dwell;
But where remorse the feelin smarts,
    Ye're neist to hell.

How cheerless shines the cheerfu light,
And lanely langsome is the night,
To mopin melancholy wight
       Wha's fancy swims,
While fiends and spectres greet his sight
       In dreary dreams?

The smiles o beauty, he may see them,
The sweets o life he canna pree them;
He sees nae things as ithers ee them:
       Trifles perplex him;
Nor music's warblin notes can please him,
       But teaze and vex him.

I've seen thy balefu influence shed
Roun skinny poortith's strawy bed;
The frienless wretch, there lowly laid,
       Thou sting'st amain,
And spread'st around his cheerless bed
       Thy gloomy train.

Till frenzied Fever's fiery han
Alang the witherin lips was drawn,
Fond Hope and Health were at a stan
       Ye crushed them there;
Then roused your daughter, wild and wan -
       E'en dark Despair!

Poor Poets, in their airy station,
Wrapt up in cobweb contemplation,
Whilst spinning out some new creation,
   Wi hopefu ee,
Are hissed by harpy Condemnation,
   Then torn by thee.

Although thy darksome gloomy reign
May cloud the thought, and sour the min,
Yet where the Bard does soarin shine,
   Wi witchin art,
Thou thrill'st the feelins there mair fine,
   And men'st the heart.

Thy gentle touch shall aften tend
To endear the lover and the friend;
To lofty reason aid thou'lt lend,
   And maxims meet,
And beauty's saftest smile wilt blend
   Wi something sweet.

Thou teachest worldly cares are vain;
Thou winn'st our thoughts frae sordid gain;
Thou gar'st us feel for ithers' pain,
   In sorrows sinkin,
And point'st frae thoughtless Folly's train
   To sober thinkin.

The Morning Invitation

Dear Chloe, why wast'st thou the moments
    That's sweetest for pleasure or health?
Thy senses are sealed up in slumbers,
    While Nature displays all her wealth.

The breath of the morning is gentle,
    And spreads with fresh fragrance the dawn;
And soft is the sound of the sea wave,
    That murmurs along on the strand.

The sun is his glories unshrouding,
    And paints with soft blushes the sky,
To banish the shades of the morning,
    And speak that his presence is nigh.

The mist's from the mountains dispelling;
    Each shepherd has sounded his horn:
The dew has bestudded the blossoms,
    That bloom on the sweet-scented thorn.

Now the trees have resumèd their clothing,
    And the small birds they sing on each spray,
As they carol their notes in the morning,
    To welcome the new coming day.

The fields they are deckèd with daisies;
    The primroses blow in the glens;
The wild lilies bud forth their blossoms,
    And violets enamel the plains.

Oh! come then, my lovely, my fairest,
    My every way charming, my queen -
Thy presence improves every landscape,
    And aids with new beauty each scene!

A wreath of the flowers I'll weave thee,
    That's sweetest for flavour and hue;
When finished as fancy shall dictate,
    I'll bind round thy polishëd brow.

On my arm I will gently support thee,
    And lead thee o'er mountains and plains;
My pipe I will sound to thee cheerily,
    And banish all care with its strains.

The far distant tops of the mountains,
    We'll mark while they're tingëd with blue;
And trees that o'ershadow the fountains -
    While our flocks are a-feeding we'll view.

Thus Nature, in her native graces,
    A charm to the mind can impart -
Beyond all the frippery of dresses,
    Or all the gay trappings of art.

The great ones may roll in their riches,
    False honour and title may prove -
But they ne'er can yield peace to the bosom,
    Like Chloe, true Friendship, and Love.

A New Song
Tune *"Green grow the Rashes, O"*

Begbie burn rins fair and clear,
    And Begbie woods are bonnie, O;
There will I wed my winsome Meg,
    If e'er I marry ony, O.
The dewy tear hangs on the briar,
    The birk and blooming thorn, O;
The cuckoo wakes the slumb'ring brake,
    And ushers in the morn, O.

Though gear be guid to him has need,
    And truly I'm but scanty, O;
Yet there's ae heart I wadna part,
    For a' yon Earl's County, O.
O Begbie woods are bonnie woods,
    And Begbie burn's sae rocky, O;
There will I wed my winsome Meg,
    Wi naething but her smoky, O.

The Old Shepherd
A Tale

The cold winds of winter did blow,
    And hissingly swept o'er the hill;
The sunbeams were sickly and low,
    As they tinged yon ice clotted mill.

'Twas down by the white clifted rock,
    Where the bare trees their branches spread wide,
Round its base nipt a poor scanty flock,
    There a hoary old Shepherd I spied.

Each feature a sorrow betrayed,
    Though his looks they betokened the sage;
His form like a bulwark decayed,
    And his head was o'ersilvered with age.

Around him a mantle of grey -
    'Twas the dye that was worn by his sheep;
At his feet lay his faithful friend, Tray,
    His charge that assisted to keep.

His hands they were withered and bare,
    That tremblingly grasped his crook;
His brow it was furrowed with care,
    While wistful and wildly he spoke.

"What is life but a trifle, a toy?
    A something, a nothing, that's gone;
As the shade of the cloud gliding by,
    Hope grasps, but the phantom is flown.

"Yet life's morning tasks, ye were sweet;
     When the bosom was vacant and gay,
How light was the sound of my feet,
     While I tuned up my pastoral lay!

"Till love from the eyes of my Ann
     Beamed forth to disquiet my mind;
But soon were my sorrows withdrawn,
     For my Anna was constant and kind.

"Though our cabin was lonely and low,
     Soft peace and content did abound;
Our labours sweet health did bestow,
     And our pledges of love were around.

"When apace our young blossoms they grew,
     My bosom exulted within,
As the striplings first guided the plough,
     And the damsel was learning to spin.

"Then fortune her gifts did unfold,
     And spread out her gay gilded train;
My flocks they increased in the fold,
     And the valleys waved wide with my grain.

"But the follies of fashion and rank, -
     The bane of the youthful and fair, -
Our offspring like honey they drank,
     And my partner was caught in the snare.

"Now our cooling brick pavement was changed
     For a cloth that must cover the floor;
In place of our milkpails arranged,
     There goblets and vases did tower.

"Our sons saw each race and each fair,
    And visits they gave and received;
'Twas confusion and bustle, and care;
    In our prospects we oft were deceived.

"The tabor beat time at the dance,
    And the Squire of the manor was there;
He deigned on our daughter to glance:
    For my Mary was thoughtless and fair.

"Alas! could I smother the rest!
    He proffered to make her his bride;
Decoyed, and then left her distrest:
    She sickened, repented, and died.

"My favourite, the son of my love,
    Was bound to a trader in town;
But the youth learned to gamble and rove,
    Till his health and his virtue were flown.

"Our oldest was haughty and vain;
    When he saw that our fortunes decreased,
He hied him far over the main,
    And left us in sorrow distrest.

"The wound of a parent's fond hope,
    My wife to her bosom has laid;
Ere her time does she wither and droop;
    And the mind's with the body decayed.

"I sigh for the friends of my youth;
    I look; but behold they are not!
Experience has taught me this truth;
    I live, yet am almost forgot.

"Like yon aged oak on the cleft,
    With bosom laid bare to each blast,
Whose branches are withered and reft,
    And leafless, and sapless, and waste.

"Thus lonely, through want and through cold,
    I tend these few sheep on the heath;
No friend to support me when old,
    To close my sad eyelids in death.

"Oh life! thou art languid to bear!
    How cheerless the prospects I see:
Though Spring shall with blossoms appear,
    She never can bud upon me.

"But why should I murmur and sigh
    At the life-cheering tints of the Spring?
Though a songster may sicken and die,
    Yet another shall carol and sing.

"Ye fields, ye shall flourish and fade,
    With your caves and your cataracts so lone;
Some shepherd more gay shall you tread,
    When my name on the hills is unknown.

"But it's cruel, ye wealthy and high,
    Thus to spill the content of the swain;
And 'tis folly in them thus to sigh
    For the rank they can never maintain."

The Peacock
A Modern Satire in Four Parts

Part 1

Gaudy bird, of gorgeous hue,
How kind has nature been to you,
In formin a your feathers fair,
Your weel fledged wings, and stars so rare,
Glancin by day, but dim by night,
Right fair for show, but dull for light.
     Like fickle friens, when Fortune twines us,
Will show their face, and proffer kindness;
But should misfortune's gloamin shade us,
We'll fin, owre late, thae friens hae fled us.
Thy gaudy neck and breast sae fine,
Where little tinted rainbows shine,
Twitterin like dewdrops on the thorn,
     When early sunbeams paint the morn.
Again thy glancin een o jet
Appear like studs in siller set;
Or pearls hung in gowden ring,
That near the ladies' luglocks hing:
Thy head appears majestic drest,
Crowned wi a bonny wavin crest;
Or like my Peggy's gumflowers gay,
That blom, although it be not May;
Or like the raw recruit's cockade,
Who thinks himsel a flashy blade,
While ribbons roun his tap he gathers,
And thinks to fear the French wi feathers;

Or dreams o gear and great preferment,
Beause he's pimpèd for his sergeant:
But lo! the hungry days o drillin,
Of marchin, haltin, floggin, wheelin,
Bow down his feathery brain o sallies,
And pluck his bonnet o its walies.

    While sprucely strutting o'er the grun,
Ye spread your beauties to the sun,
And veer about wi airy pride,
To keep afore your fairest side;
Or jink aroun wi airy wheel,
To hide the bareness o your keel.

    So busked beau, around the ring,
Will flirt and ogle, dance and sing;
Wi dashing wig o mony a shade,
To grace him when his hair is fled;
Displays his snuffbox, hands a fan,
And shows himsel a lady's man:
But should he deign the dance to wheel up,
Or miss a foot, and cock his keel up,
What dire disgrace might intervene,
And a his lockless lugs be seen!

    Alas! for human nature's frail!
A peacock soon may lose his tail:
Yet comin spring wi genial heat,
Can mak the bird again complete:
But beaux may tine, and few to see them,
What belles or barbers ne'er can gie them.

    What gars ye flutter roun your hens?
Ye'll dirty a your bonny pens;
And raise a stour might spoil your gloss,
And gar your beauties come to loss.
Is that the way ye show your passion,

Or is't the method now in fashion? -
I truly think it is the gait,
For yonder's ane taen wi the bait.
　　　Ah, Meg, wert thou as kind to me -
Fa in my arms thus for a wee,
I'd hae mysel wi feathers stuck,
And for thy sake become a buck.
　　　Thus fools o fashion spread their lures,
And dashin show their outward powers;
Will shake their frills wi fuss and din,
But, O! it's vacuum a within.
Yet thick and thrang are Folly's bairns,
That will be caught by outward charms.
How soon we see some female pet,
And like the Peahen catch the bait.
　　　So theatre nymph in borough town,
Wi silken hose and glancin gown,
That's no distressed wi meikle happin,
Disclose the beauties o her crappin;
And should that fail, she'll dance a jig,
To shaw the shinside o her leg,
Keen to entrap some merchant loon,
Or countra laird new come to town.
Her capper clippins glister fine,
He never saw ought sae divine;
Wi love he's like to break his shins,
To win a wee ayont the screens:
He casts a wink, she's kirr and couth,
And draws the water to his mouth,
Then at the lang run pumps his purse, -
Great mercy gif it be nae worse! -
Syne draws the curtain roun her spark,
Where love works wonders in the dark.

I never saw, but I've heard say
(Folks see not wonders ilka day),
And doubtna ye hae a heard tell,
O peacocks wi a fiery tail,
Might show a man his goods to hanle,
And save him meikle coal and canle.
So, haply, he may fin bestowed,
Some sure memorial for his gowd.
'Tis thus declining female star,
That tines her blossom in the war;
Wha's beauty's worn to shreds and patches,
When nature fails, at art she catches;
Rubs o'er wi reams her brows and mouth -
Like longlived birds renews her youth.
Her cheeks turned pale, supplies wi paint,
Still breath she smoors wi oils and mint;
E'en Nature's knowes that now are fled,
Where love in youthfu days has played,
She'll them supply wi teats o woo,
That cheat the unsuspecting view:
Yet though they hum the gazing youth,
A near encounter shows the truth.
Some forward spark, on midnight ramble,
Descries their fauts but coal or canle.
But O! sic borrowed charms are frail:
'Tis whispered roun, her lovers fail;
She now leaves balls and sic-like places,
And scours to fairs and countra races,
Wi ruffs and muffs, and trappins mony,
To hook some simple countra Johnny.
But countra John likes countra Jenny,
And nane taks tent o gentle Fanny.
Wi dust gets a her walies spoiled,

Or may be waur, her wishes foiled,
She fears her freaks are near an en,
And pines awa like "Jinken's hen":
Yet still she sighs for youthfu sport,
And now she tries the last effort.
Wi haly reverence in her looks,
She buys a bunch o preachin beuks;
And o the faith becomes defendant,
And lives a pious independent:
Wi former friens has mony a battle,
But they like nae sic cantin cattle.
Till some pert lad that lives by weavin
Her mim-moud looks and sighs deceivin,
Mistaks for grace her whines and rantin,
She traps him by the bait o cantin.

Now some may say this is a gay joke,
Comparin ladies to a peacock.
Can sic-like rhymers and pretenders,
That's lost their reckonin in the genders,
Set up their face wi men o letters,
To spin out satires on their betters;
Wi crabbit mou our fauts to hammer?
They'd better stap and learn their grammar.

But I can tell my learned readers,
For a their skill in tropes and figures,
'Tis better than to seek assistance,
Frae beings that ne'er had existence.
There's mony a lengthened learned head,
Has spun out rhymes for fools to read,
Wi heathen gods and fictions drest,
Syrens and Sylphs, and a the rest -
Gif pick out thae from every nook,
Their rhymes might gang in little bouk.

Poets o panegyric or satire,
Hae studied fiction mair than nature:
So I, like them, may look about me,
I seek hyperboles to suit me.

Part 2

But still my story is nae done yet -
Perhaps the maist o't is to come yet
So here I go, be't verse or prose,
To draw my similies to a close.
But faith I fear I've tint my subject,
And wi my fancies lost the object;
My bird is no yet full surveyed,
We'll view him on the other side.
      E'en thou, wi a thy outward shape,
Thy studded tail and glossy nape,
Hast e'en thy failings, cracks and flaws,
Thy eldritch scraichs and fiend-like claws:
Thy belly's but a dirty din,
Thy flesh and banes are foul within;
As I hae seen a stately biggin,
Restin aboon the great folks riggin,
Contrived by pride to rot in state,
Engraved wi mighty, lofty, great;
But search it closely, lo, ye'll fin
But banes and dust and dross within.
      But something whispers, Haud ye there!
In this ye dinna reason fair:
Your wame's fu weel for a our blethers,
Although it has nae bonny feathers;
They hap you weel and keep you warm,
And save your tenderer parts frae harm.

So things we never should abuse,
That's no for show, but made for use -
There's ither birds that I could name,
Has coarser feathers on their wame;
And mony a fowl, though brawly tappit,
That looks best when their legs are happit.
  But then, again, pray what's your use?
Ye're seen about nae poor man's house -
Ye're no for travel, no for toilin,
Ye're no for roastin, stewin, boilin
Your only being's but for show,
Or mind the ladies o a beau.
Are ye contenter wi your pens,
Than cock-malierie wi his hens,
While he upon the midden craws,
And ye to sun spread out your braws?
Or can ye better bide the stour
Of comin winter's chilly power;
Or dree misfortune's keener storm,
Than chucky in her hamely form?
I trow your trappins then are vain,
And only catch the win and rain;
And rather prove a source of sorrows -
But 'las! thou hast owre mony marrows.
  Nature through a her various roads,
Bestows nae pleasure wi sic odds,
As whiles we think, in lowly state,
Viewin the greatness o the great;
For if content's within the breast,
Eneugh will do as weel's a feast:
'Tis true they hae the brawer houses,
Their naigs, and nowte, and rowth o spouses;
Their chaise to ride in when they tire -

Their ease, their wine, their bleezin fire;
Their titles, lands, and livins braw,
Their crouchin flunkies at their ca;
Their sumptuous meals are never scant,
They never ken the carle, Want -
But then, what signifies their treasure?
Their burden Plenty brings nae pleasure;
They're born to wealth, and think't nae blessin;
They ken nae pleasure in possessin.
Gif nae restraint the object claim,
It leaves the wish without an aim.
Idle in life, they try a schemes,
Adorn their backs, and fill their wames;
Fulfil ilk wish, be't right or wrang,
But never stay by ae thing lang.
They ken nae gude o weel-timed meal,
That kitchens oft the poor man's kail;
They never ken the sweets o toilin,
That keeps the gloomy mind frae spoilin;
They're seldom blest wi rosy health,
For a their lumps o ease and wealth;
Or virtuous love and bairnies roun,
That keep the feeble hopes in tune.
In short, we've thoughtless joys and wants,
They wealth, wi nervous thraws and gaunts.
        Though flauntin, for a slight inspection,
Ye downa thole a close dissection;
And thus the proverb does declare,
That far aff fowls hae feathers fair.
Again, we hae the sage's word,
That feathers often form the bird;
But twine thee o thy trappins a,
Thou'rt waur faurd than a pluckit daw.

Now, should our men o holy order,
Be strippit o their bands and border,
And sic-like trappins o the sect,
That draws a reverence o respect;
Tak aff the mystic wig and cloak,
A priest might look like ither folk.
His face or flank indeed might shine -
Though no wi guzzlin beef or wine;
But by the grace beams frae within,
Or blushin for his country's sin;
Or knops on's knees, worn hard as horn,
Wi lengthened kneelins night and morn.
Aiblins, through sleep's forgetfu potion,
The foul thief whiles might draw his notion,
When reason's pores and doors are steekit,
To dream o glebes and stipens eekit,
And ither things there's nae great harm in,
As wenches, manses, horns, or farmin;
Or guns, or gloves, or ither whims -
But wha can answer for their dreams?

So Soldier shape in scarlet dashes,
Wi sword-knots, tassels, cane, and sashes;
Wi frills and feathers on his tappin,
He flegs through a the nooks o Wappin,
Some tailor loon or pander spark,
That made his court to Lucky C- - k.
But should some former shopmate meet him,
And thus in cantin dialect greet him:
"What, neighbour Snip! upon my word,
He's changed his bodkin for a sword;
Though thread and thimble low do lie,
The 'goose,' I see, is fit to fly:
If duly taught, may answer soon,

For an invasion of the moon."
He'd prance and stare - "Why, demme, I
Never knew thee, thou chattering pye.
Decamp, or by my bloody weapons,
I'll cut thy buckram soul to shapins!"
Then ruthless draws his glancin rapier,
And round his comrade cuts a caper.
But should the route direct his courses
To join afar his country's forces;
Or battle burst and him but hear o't,
He'd faint and fa wi perfect fear o't;
There bloodless lie amang the slain,
And wish him at his wark again.

So Dominies, wi great pretences,
Because they're up to verbs and tenses,
And 'cause bairns cower, and ca them Master,
And 'cause they use the lance and clyster;
Alike in every science happy,
To pluck a tooth or set a capy;
Think they can judge o verse or prose,
And pert pop in their word and nose;
Will tell you a what's right, what's wrang;
How this line's short, and that line's lang;
Yet ken nae mair o fancy's power
Than Peacocks, kickin up a stour.

And Lawyers, too, that brazen tribe,
That tak nae pains their fauts to hide,
Like Pharaoh's lean kye, hard they bite,
And live upon their neibour's spite. -
To paint their pranks I'm nae proficien:
We'll try some easier acquisition.

Part 3

Again my bird, we'll try to find
The matchless beauties o your mind.
Frae ither fowls ye stan abeigh,
And, like a fools, wad fain be high:
Proud, on a wa, or half-grown tree,
Or chimly tap, ye like to be;
There cock your crest, wi airy show,
And squint on scrapin birds below.

But should the sky begin to lower,
And wake your second-sighted power,
Ye then disclose your cowardly failins,
And grate a roun you wi your yellins.
Nae croakin raven, wi his note,
Can equal what comes through your throat;
Nor clamorous cats, wham midnight summons,
Can equal half your yells and omens.
Ye fright the heron where he flies,
And weary Echo wi your cries.

So hae I seen great fuss and caperin
'Mang mystic knighthood o the apron;
Wi empty pride, in monkish gown,
Travish a Bible through the town:
Wi painted poles and pictured duds,
And aprons new come frae the suds,
Or stunted frae the wife's sark tail -
Aiblins the pock that hauds his meal;
For H-r-m's sons hae mony wants,
For a their outward shows and rants,
Though patronised by weeds and saints.
The lengthened legends, tales, and histories,
And dark sublime Egyptian mysteries,

Are kindly meant, by your designment,
To draw the warld to refinement.
Your mystic draughts, wi keel and cauk,
Gar mony a cudroch chiel to quak;
Joinin some green-horn for a blether,
Ye light his purse and een thegither;
Then roun him ring, and prance, and squeel,
To gar folks trow ye raise the deil:
But deil a deil wad show his face,
Sic bare-faced mummery e'er to grace.
Yet gie nae way to dark despondence,
Although the deils deny attendance;
Though lazy Cloots sits still within,
Ye'll aiblins grape the way to him;
Where ye may herd in future times,
Unscaithed by ony Cowan's rhymes.
　　So drover blades, wha drink and sot,
Wha's light's confined to stirk and stot,
That's scraped their gear frae lowly stations,
Wi quirks, and breaks, and sequestrations,
Club roun, and tell their loathsome jokes,
Or plot to cheat douce countra folks;
Wi arle-penny in their han,
Will belch out something like a d- n,
How that's the highest groat they'll gie,
And be mansworn thrice in a day,
Then mount, and hame, wi saucy gloom:
Ilk likes to ride his neighbour down,
Because he has an Irish horse,
And ithers' gowd within his purse.
　　So countra Laird, that's stout and frisky,
Bred up 'mang grooms, and drinkin whisky
And footin't fairly o'er the bogs,

Pursuing hares and hounding dogs;
Taught by his mither that his talents
Surpasses ither countra callants,
Scours aff, ne'er dreaming on defection,
And buys the votes at neist election;
Syne up to London in a wheel,
And thinks himsel a clever chiel.
In House o Commons glowers and gaunts,
And langs to tell his countra's wants
Or rather show his pert essays,
So, like a jack-ass, starts and brays;
And what in point o sense is lackin
He'll eith supply wi stamps and brakin.
I kenna how it comes to pass,
But court folks whiles will keep an ass;
Whether for ridin or for milk,
Or length o lugs, I kenna whilk;
They'll hear their cracks, and ne'er confute them;
They'll bear their kicks, and ne'er dispute them.
    Thus hae I seen a simple lad,
Amang the braes o Galloway bred,
If no o'ergane wi information,
At least quite free frae affectation,
When siller lured or wark was slack,
Cross Bowness burn to bear a pack;
There serve a time, but gowd or fee,
To learn, to cheat, and gab, and lie;
Schooled by some greedy, gripin elf,
To smother every tie but self,
Till by degrees he learns the knack
Of logic, how to blaw the pack:
Though aft his traffic and resort
Is but amang the baser sort.

Yet hame he comes, baith proud and braw,
His new acquirements fair to shaw,
In Lonon boots and broad-brimmed hat,
Wi yeas and nays, and G- d knows what;
Queer whirrs and burrs, eneugh to fley folk,
Wi a the scum o Yorkshire dialect. -
He d- s the reek, and rubs his een,
And tells what unco sights he's seen.
His mither ees her hopefu lad,
And thinks him truly learned and bred.
        Bright similies might here be spun,
In number like motes i the sun,
And on the mind so thick lie fraught,
As maks ane dizzy wi the thought.

Part 4

Now see what passion rules thy heart,
And how thou act'st the parent's part.
If a be true that I've heard said,
Ye're but a vile ungratefu blade:
Ye daut your dames through a the year,
Till ance the clockin time draws near,
Then if ane wanders frae the rest,
To hatch her young or right her nest,
Ye follow in your surly flegs,
And paik the hen and break the eggs,
Then leave her pained in waesome manner,
Her liefu lane through woods to waner,
Till sair for-fought wi grief and pinin,
She finds a nest ayont your kennin;
A twig o hazel's a her happin,
To hatch her young wi hungry crappin,

There tossed by wind and beat wi rain:
But Hope, that soothes the parent's pain,
Calms a the sorrows o her breast,
And points wi pleasure to her nest.
  Parental kindness, child o Nature,
That warms the breast o every creature,
Beeted by feelins finest fires,
Unstained by ony base desires,
Thou maks ilk' bein kind and heedfu,
As lang as Nature sees it's needfu,
Savin the scum o earth accurst;
Wha's ends are sordid gain and lust.
  Yet thou in this art no thy lane, -
To seek for pleasure without pain;
To like the night, but shun the day,
To hate the toil, but like the play.
So baudrons likes the trout to eat,
But downa think to douk her feet;
So patriots for their country's glory,
Will act the Whig, and hate the Tory;
Will raise a lengthened learned digression,
On law, and rights, and constitution;
Will stand by liveries and petitions,
And rail at wars and expeditions. -
As lang's the birkie wants a place,
Or untaen tent o by His Grace -
E'en then he'll whiles pay some attention,
Till fairly tongue-tacked wi a pension;
He'll then sit down amang the monniest,
And think the braidest road the bonniest,
Syne leaves his countra, where he got her -
Mang wants and woes and war to swatter.
  Thus countra lasses, void o care,

Like water lilies, saft and fair,
When love's within and charms without them,
Like flies the lads will buzz about them;
While each his art and fortune tries,
The fausest aften wins the prize:
For mony a merry tale he'll speak,
To keep the dimple on her cheek;
Brings claps and squeezes to's assistance -
For what are words when at a distance? -
Then tells the same dull story o'er,
That he has said to mony a score -
As how she kills him wi her glances,
That cut his heart-strings through like lances;
Swears by his saul he doesna flout her;
And that he canna live without her;
That she, wha has the power to save,
Should deign some pity to her slave -
At least, to let him live in hope,
And no, at ance, his breath to stop:
"Whaeer is dearest to this breast -
He surely maun be truly blest;"
Then steals a kiss, looks in her ee,
And thinks she'll hardly let him die.
Sic ravings gars her bosom heave -
'Tis woman's province to believe
And a her kind that e'er I kent o,
Are fully fond to be ta'en tent o.
    It needs sma foresight what's to follow,
Or how his sensual saul and hollow,
Stoops down below the rax o truth,
To cheat her unsuspecting youth;
And when her feckless virtue's gane,
She's left to sab and greet her lane:

I've seen her reaved o a her charms,
Her helpless affspring in her arms,
Wi few to ask her how she fares,
Or sooth her grief or share her cares;
Despised, in want, and deep distress,
Gars a her feelings bleed afresh.

But wha can paint the parent's woes,
Whas breast wi piercing sorrow throes -
Their joy, where a their hopes were centred,
Owre far on faithless seas has ventured?
Haply the parent's lowly laid,
That reared wi care the luckless maid.
Then mae will toy and praise her beauty,
Than teach the thoughtless maid her duty,
Till left at large to passion's snare,
That aften leads to dark despair. -
When, lost to notice, lost to shame,
She dares the deed we darena name.

Alas! where's a thy beauties now,
Thy dimpled cheek and cherry mou -
The takin twinkles o your een,
The maiden blush and modest mien -
The matchless ringlets o your hair,
Might made a moderate face look fair -
That native note, of tunefu glee,
That carried aye the charm to me -
And simple kindness without art,
That never failed to touch the heart? -
They're feckly fled, what could prevent them?
And those still left hae few to tent them.

Beauty, though sages sair dispute thee,
Poets like aye to rhyme about thee.
Thou cheer'st the heart when'er we see thee,

And fettered fancy canna leave thee;
Thou plead'st thy cause in silent looks,
Better than orators or books;
Canst smooth the brow o gloomy thought,
And set our re-resolves at nought.
Gif weel adorned wi truth and love,
Thou'd picture a the joys above;
For what has life to gie that's sweeter,
To make our earthly joys completer?
Yet aft thou'st been a great transgressor,
And proved a bane to the possessor -
Hast fostered pride and marred instruction,
And robbed the mind by deep deduction;
A sign-post set to gather knaves,
And ruins ten for twa thou saves:
Then, Oh! - but stop, where's this I'm gaun?
My story's surely fully lang;
So here my similies shall cease,
And let my readers rest in peace,
To rax their banes and rub their een,
For fear they fret and tak the spleen -
Only, I'd slightly wish to mention,
How, that it ne'er was my intention
To point at ony trade or callin,
Or triumph in a neibour's failin:
For, 'las! we always fin't owre true,
We're a possessed o fau'ts enow:
But, as for fashion's silly tools,
And empty, dull, conceited fools,
That seem to tell us, by their ways,
That sauls o men are shown in claes;
And wit and worth and a respects,
Are tacked to certain sorts and sects

It shall not hurt my expectation,
Although I want their approbation;
And should some passage pet or pout them,
They ken best if the bonnet suit them.
There's mony mae I haena noted,
Deserve't as weel as those hae got it:-
For selfish pride and affectation,
Hae spread their wings sae o'er the nation,
That scarce a vestige now ye'll see,
O what like mankin ought to be -
Like beggar's cloak o Bethnal Green,
Wha's origin could scarce be seen: -
But time would fail me - here I'll en,
And leave them to some abler pen;
Or try mysel, some future time,
When I'm again disposed for rhyme.

Peggy
Tune *"Swaggering, Roaring Willie"*

When first I foregathered wi Peggy,
 My Peggy and I were young;
Sae blythe at the bught i the gloamin
 My Peggy and I hae sung.
 My Peggy and I hae sung,
Till the stars did blink sae hie;
Come weel or come woe to the beggin,
 My Peggy was dear to me.

The stately aik stood on the mountain,
 And towered o'er the green birken shaw;
Ilk glentin wee flower on the meadow,
 Seemed proud o bein buskit sae braw.
 Seemed proud o bein buskit sae braw
When they saw their ain shape i the Dee;
'Twas there that I courted my Peggy,
 Till the kirk it fell foul o me.

Though love it has little to look for
 Frae the heart that is wedded to gear;
A wife without house or a hadden
 Gars ane look right blate like and queer.
 Gars ane baith look blate like and queer,
But queerer when twa turns to three;
Our friens they hae foughten and flyten,
 But Peggy's aye dear to me.

It vexed me her sighin and sabbin,
    Now nought aniest marriage would do;
And though that our prospects were dreary,
    What could I but e'en buckle to?
    What could I but e'en buckle to,
And dight the saut tear frae her ee?
The warl's a wearifu wister
    But Peggy's aye dear to me.

Rural Retirement

Oh! Rural Life, thou blest retreat,
    Where sweet contentment dwells aye;
To me ye're dearer than the street,
    Where din and discord yells aye.
There, countless wretches are immured,
    In fell disease and starvin'
And thrivin' knaves to guilt inured,
    Frae virtue's paths are swervin.

Right dear to me are glens and howes,
    Wi craigs aboon me towerin,
While burns come tumblin frae the knowes,
    And owre the linns are pourin.
The sun blinks blythely on the pool,
    That bickers to his glances;
There water clocks, untaught by rule,
    Skip through their countra dances.

The sturdy aik aboon the brow,
    Supports the feeble ivy;
See how it twines wi mony a bow,
    Just as it were alive aye.
The bloomin broom, the hawthorn white,
    That scents the caller mornin,
And wild flowers that the heart delight,
    The banks and brows adornin.

Here blythesome birds on hazel boughs,
    Chant up their mornin ditty;
Amang the firs the cushat coos, -
    Hear how she wails sae pretty!
Better they relish Nature's laws,
    Than man wi a his knowledge,
And fill their place, but cracks or flaws,
    Though ne'er at school or college.

The sheep, amang the bracken braes,
    Are feedin wi their lammies;
There, kids as white as new bleached claes,
    'Mang crags bleat for their mammies.
The shepherd lad sae blythe and gay,
    Does loudly tune his chanter;
Plays "Owre the hills and far away,"
    To chase ilk care and canker.

Yet still the bonniest flower's unsung
        O a creation's plantin;
For thee has mony a harp been strung,
        And ilka heart been pantin;
But if the precious dew o sense
        Bedeck't, it shows the sweeter;
Fostered by mirthfu modest mense,
        It maks the gift completer.

Leeze me on e'en, when hill and tree
        Are pictured in the vallies;
When lassies to the loan do hie,
        To milk and feed their mailies;
While sweet and lang they lilt the sang,
        As lads come frae the mawin,
Wha pree their mou ere it be lang,
        In corner till the dawin.

When seated roun the milkin slap,
        Their toils are a forgotten:
For lasses' looks hae aye the knack
        To stir up fun and jokin.
The lads that's kind will bear the pail,
        And pair as love directs them;
While lightly footin't owre the dale,
        Nae doubts or fears perplex them.

Now e'ening star to lovers dear,
    Beams in the purple east;
Wi modest beauties saft and clear,
    Like Peggy's spotless breast.
The moon like ony buskëd bride,
    In siller grey was glancin,
And on the restless rocking tide
    Her lightsome locks were dancin.

But sure Contentment lives, hersel,
    Beneath yon braw clay biggin,
Weel theekit frae the heathery fell,
    While brackens crown the riggin.
The honeysuckles speel the roof,
    And fouse adorn the gavel;
The frienly firs, they keep it noof,
    Frae Boreas' baulest devel.

Here, glancin trenchers in a raw,
    And luggies laid in order;
There stuff-hung bed, fu doucely braw,
    Fringed featly roun the border.
The sattle chair, for seat or bed,
    Wi forms and tables scoured weel,
And glancin green-horns snugly laid,
    In Lucky Dad's ain spoon-creel.

Here auld folks live wi bairns' bairns,
    And blest wi peace and plenty;
Here, parents' hope the bosom warms,
    Here youth blooms fair and dainty:
Here dwell the mither's virtuous smiles,
    The faithfu friend and father;
Unlike them skilled in city wiles,
    That aften slip the tether.

Here grey-beard mirth forgets his years,
    And tells his tale fu cheerly;
Amazed, the listening youngster hears
    The feats o Papish Charlie.
But when the lasses tune the lays,
    As Coila's Bard composed them;
'Bout thoughtless joys o lover's waes,
    They dirl through the bosom.

What though they hae nae opera joys,
    Or carriage gay to flaunt in;
Or dainty that the stomach cloys,
    They never ken they want em.
Their hame-spun grey, and halesome fare,
    Mak life as sweet's the gentry's;
And what they hae, they freely share,
    Nor heed they learned comment'ries.

Unknown to them the borrowed glance,
    To smile when sorrows twine them;
Or a the mummeries come frae France:
    Few spleens or vapours pine them.
There life is like yon toddlin burn;
    Though cross craigs whiles may stint it,
Still presses owre ilk thrawart turn,
    And never looks behint it.

My wearied limbs I'd here repose,
    And woo the muses roun me;
There mark the briar that bears the rose,
    While lav'rocks tower aboon me.
Here, far frae busy bustlin strife,
    I'd tend life's latest ember;
Unteased by feignèd friends or wife,
    That wauken care and clamour.

On Siller

Oh! Siller, but thou costs us dear,
By ony ither kind o gear!
Now, fient a ane thy price need speer,
        But knaves or fools;
For few can e'er thy price come near -
        By honest rules.

Thou gars Religion tine her haud;
Maks her a slow, saft-fingered jade;
And looses Folly, ravin mad
        Wi pride and nonsense;
Maks honest Honour sick and sad,
        And smoors poor Conscience.

For thee we sell our finest feelins -
Pity and Love, thae gentle yealins;
E'en sacred Friendship gets her drillins,
        Though deep imprest;
And feigns her flame wi bows and kneelins,
        For self-int'rest.

For thee we toil baith night and day,
Till bluid turns thin and locks grow grey,
And ither dools, in dark array,
        Aroun us muster;
And crazy joints to climb life's brae -
        A weary wister.

For thee I crossed my youthfu fancy,
Forsook my bloomin smilin Nancy,
And pud a docken for a tansy,
   And cursed my life
Wi tap o a things maist unchancy -
   A haverel wife!

My haill designs she's aye for balkin
When I'm for peace, then she's for talkin;
When dull, she skirls like a maukin,
   And laughs and girns:
When I'm for sleepin, she's for waukin,
   And peels my shins.

Then, gif she getna a' her will,
She feigns her fits, flytes, and fas ill;
To a her neibours roun does tell
   How ill I'm till her;
And aye the owre-word o the knell,
   Her waefu siller!

Now, every comfort I maun tine -
The joys o wit, the joys o wine,
The chimes o music and o rhyme,
   And comrades dear,
And thole her loud eternal whine
   About her gear.

Let never better be his weird,
Each social tie that could discard
For glancin gowd, or dirty yird,
      Or empty fame:
May cankered Care tug at his beard,
      And sullen dame.

But L- d, gif ance her head were hidden,
I'se ne'er again be woman-ridden;
My former friens should a be bidden,
      In social ring
The dool-string I should soon get rid on,
      And dance and sing!

The Soldier's Home
A Tale

Where yon grey rocks resist the flood
      On Scotia's southern strand,
I saw, in melancholy mood,
      A rustic veteran stand.

Silent he gazed on sea and shore;
      High towered the village smoke,
The sun hard on his temples bore,
      While thus he silence broke -

"Here musing o'er the lapse of time,
      Since thoughtless childhood played,
And ripening manhood's youthful prime
      In stately steps had strayed.

"Imagination fondly roves,
     Where cares and ills were few,
And pictures all our joys and loves,
     And hopes and fears anew.

"The long lost youthful friend we view,
     Bedecked with heartfelt smiles,
And tenderer ties of love review,
     With all her witching wiles.

"With caution now each step we tread,
     And trace each haunt with care;
But youth is flown, and friends are fled:
     Alas! she dwells not there.

"Though fair each streamlet still does flow,
     And wider spread the trees;
Yet by some cause they waken woe -
     Ceased is their power to please.

"A stranger occupies the cot
     Where first my being grew,
A rude, unpolished, selfish sot,
     With all his gaping crew.

"One friend, that sighed for fortune large,
     To foreign lands has sped;
A dearer left his lonely charge,
     And laid him with the dead.

"Thoughts fond and vain the mind employ -
    We're borne along the stream;
The bud of life is all a toy,
    Its wane a weary dream.

"My first fond love in life's fair morn,
    By luckless love undone,
Retiring far from public scorn
    Has reared her only son.

"Why left I what my soul held dear,
    To sigh in crowds alone?
'Twas siren Hope sung in mine ear,
    And flattering, soothed me on.

"Dear Mary, though for fame and gold
    The battle blade I've borne,
Lo! here I come, more poor, more old,
    More wretched and forlorn.

"But shall not we join hand in hand,
    Our wayward fate to bear,
And closer bind each former band,
    And wipe each falling tear?

"Prosperity may well afford
    A beam to glad the breast;
But ne'er could touch the tender chord,
    Like mutual love distrest.

"Welcome ye distant hills and heath,
          Though barren, rude, and bare;
My Mary's smile shall smooth each path,
          And sooth the brow of care."

Thus sung the soldier, worn with toil
          His country's shield and spear;
With mingled passions marked the soil,
          Untrod for many a year.

Though pointed pebbles on the way
          Assailed his weary feet;
The wild bird carolled loud his lay,
          And cheered him up the steep.

But when the destined booth he reached,
          Where jutting crags were seen,
A silver lake its bosom stretched,
          And wild woods waving green.

Quick beat his heart with fondest joy,
          He gazed, he viewed them o'er;
His Mary, by his favourite boy,
          Sat knitting near the door.

What though fleet time with paler hue
          Her youthful bloom had foiled,
Within her eye of azure blue,
          Content and kindness smiled.

His manly visage soon she knew,
　　Though hacked in war's alarms,
She rose, she gazed, and breathless flew
　　Into his longing arms.

As wept the father o'er his child,
　　Whose absence long he mourned,
Such joys might angels, undefiled,
　　Feel when a soul's returned.

There did he rest his wearied frame,
　　And tells his tales of war;
His boy delights to hear the theme,
　　And marks each honest scar.

A father's fondest care is used,
　　Each virtue to commend,
Till, by degrees, he now has lost
　　The father in the friend.

Such are the hopes, the joys of age,
　　That cheer life's waning ray;
More sure than all that stoic sage,
　　And lettered pride display.

Song
Tune *"Nae Dominies for me, Laddie"*

Again the breeze blaws through the trees;
    The flowers bloom by the burn, Willie:
Gay Spring is seen in fairy green -
    The year nae mair shall mourn, Willie.

The tender buds hang on the woods,
    And lowly slaethorn tree, Willie;
Its blossom spreads, nor cauld blast dreads,
    But may be nipt like me, Willie.

The frienless hare is chased nae mair,
    She whids alang the lea, Willie:
Through dewy showers the lav'rock towers,
    And sings, but not for me, Willie.

When frae thy arms, a nature's charms,
    What pleasure can they gie, Willie?
My Spring is past, my sky o'ercast,
    It's sleepless nights wi me, Willie.

Silent and shy, they now gae by,
    That used to speak wi me, Willie;
Nae tale, nae sang, the hale day lang -
    Its a for lovin thee, Willie.

Wi wily art ye wan my heart -
    That heart nae mair is free, Willie:
Then, oh! be kind, sin now it's thine!
    I had nae mair to gie, Willie.

But vain I've pled, for thou hast wed
    A wealthier bride than me, Willie;
Now nought can heal the wound I feel,
    But lay me down and die, Willie.

Fareweel ye braes, and happier days!
    By crystal windin Cree, Willie,
When o'er my grave the green grass waves,
    Oh! wilt thou think on me, Willie?

Song

High mantles the reek o the village gay,
    As the sun sinks in the west;
As pensive and slow by the meadow I stray,
    To muse on the maid I loe best.

And dear is the hum of the village bairns,
    At evening as they play;
It is borne on the wing of the gloaming gale,
    And wafted far away.

And fair and sweet are the village maids,
    As they lightly trip the green;
But the air and the grace of my lovely young Jess,
    Proclaim her the village queen.

Soft, soft is her smile as the blush of May,
    When morning purples the sky;
And wild are the tones of her witching voice
    As the Zephyr of spring sweeping by.

Like a ray of the morn are her yellow locks,
    O'ershading a bosom of love;
And saft shoots the beam o her bonny blue eye
    As the glance o the timid dove.

I've promised to lead her to the hazel shaw,
    When the sun rides high at noon;
And cheer her lone hours wi the fondest love tales,
    Till the broad flaming orb gangs down.

I've promised to pu her the wilding rose,
    The daisy and the blue-bell,
To weave a love wreath her tresses to braid,
    By the brink of the fairy well.

I've sworn by the smile that dwells on her lip,
    And the sparkle that lives in her ee,
That till baith are quenched by the damps o death
    I true to her will be.

Song
(by T.C.)
Tune *"Jackson's Cog in the Morning"*

O! Come my dear lassie wi me to the green,
The clover does bud and the daisy is seen -
Remember the promise that ye made yestreen,
        To tak a walk out i the mornin:
The sun's golden beams saftly gildeth the morn;
The birds sweetly chantin their notes frae the thorn:
The dew draps are hingin sae clear on the corn,
        An sweet smells the flow'rs i the mornin.

Yet still there is something that's dearer to me:
The rose o thy cheek, and the blink o thy ee,
Through ilk cross an care they aye comfort woud gie,
        An cheer me baith e'enin an mornin:
The king wi his crown, or the duke wi his star,
May elbow for honour or counsel for war:
Sic cares bring but crosses - I'm happier far
        When walkin wi you i the mornin.

The beauties o Simmer can please while 'tis May,
Yet, how frail is their form, and how short is their stay?
So youth wi its blossoms will shortly decay -
        E'en thy charms will but last like the mornin:
But wat ye what pleasures the bosom can yield,
When love's saft impression true friendship has seal'd,
Frae the cauld blasts o fortune 'twould ay be a bield;
        An cheer us baith e'nin an mornin?

*Note: The reference to T.C is unclear - perhaps it refers to
Thomas Cunninghame (1766-1834). M M Harper leaves
this poem out of later editions.*

Song
Tune *"Will ye walk the woods with me?"*

Oh! will ye go to yon burn side,
    Amang the new made hay,
And sport upon the flowery swaird,
    My ain dear May?

The sun blinks blythe on yon burn side,
    Where lambkins lightly play,
The wild bird whistles to his mate,
    My ain dear May.

The waving woods, wi mantle green,
    Shall shield us in the bower,
Where I'll pu a posy for my May,
    O mony a bonny flower.

My father maws ayont the burn,
    My mammy spins at hame;
And should they see thee here wi me,
    I'd better been my lane.

The lightsome lammie little kens
    What troubles it await -
When ance the flush o spring is o'er,
    The fause bird leaes its mate.

The flowers will fade, the woods decay,
    And lose their bonny green;
The sun wi clouds may be o'ercast,
    Before that it be e'en.

Ilk thing is in its season sweet;
    So love is, in its noon;
But cankering Time may foil the flower,
    And spoil its bonny bloom.

Oh! come then while the summer shines,
    And love is young and gay;
Ere age his withering, wintry blast
    Blaws o'er me and my May.

For thee I'll tend the fleecy flocks,
    Or haud the halesome plough,
And nightly clasp thee to my breast,
    And prove aye leal and true.

The blush o'erspread her bonny face,
    She had nae mair to say,
But gae her hand and walked alang,
    The youthfu bloomin May.

Song
Tune *"Roving Irishman"*

While roving round the banks of Cree,
    Seeking a strayëd ewe and lamb,
The day was dry, no one was nigh,
    The water smooth, the breezes calm.

The flowers sprung wanton by the burn;
    Up through the glen the mavis sang;
I leaned me by yon birken bower,
    And feared no ill from any man.

But by there came a blythesome youth,
    That lightly tripped along the way;
His locks were like the raven's wing,
    His look bespoke a bosom gay.

Soon as he spied me in the shade,
    Upon his step he made a stand,
So wilily he looked at me,
    And gently took me by the hand.

Said he, "Fair maid, the sun is high,
    I've long wished for the cooling shade; -
I hope ye'll not offended be
    At this small freedom I have made.

"May ill befall his cruel heart,
    Such blooming beauty could trepan:
Be easy, dear, you need not fear,
    I am no rakish Irishman.

So sweet his looks - so smooth his tongue-
    His graceful form so straight and tall;
He clasped my waist, my lips he prest;
    Alas! my heart believèd all!

From Glasgow town he said he came,
    That wealth and beauty doth comman;
'Twas then my ear - too late, I fear,
    Perceived the roving Irishman.

My Mother wonders why I'm sad:
    On May-day last I skipped and sang;
My sister says my bloom's decayed;
    I sigh and sab the whole night lang.

The time's gone by he should been here;
    My feeble hopes are near a stan:
Ye maids on Cree, be ruled by me -
    Ne'er trust a roving Irishman!

Song
Tune *"Bonny Dundee"*

Where are the joys that I felt in life's morning?
    Where are the moments once pleasing to me?
With fortune's gay graces that fluttered around me,
    Gay as the sun-beam that blinks on the lee:

Why heaves my heart with this high throbbing sorrow?
    Why soothing hope from my bosom thus flown;
Why is this visage so pale and dejected,
    With eyes overflowin an fix'd on the groun?

Is it for Nature, that's naked an ravag'd,
    By rough wintry blasts as they scowl o'er the plain?
The sun will return, with his beams more endearing,
    Soon will bring Nature her simmer again.

But what though the fields in their verdure shall flourish,
    With birds sweetly chanting their notes frae the tree,
They ne'er can revive the lone bosom from mourning,
    Or bring my dear Willie again back to me!

Aft through these groves wi my Willie I've wander'd;
    Simmer was cheerfu, an Nature was gay:
Now as I wander the night it is eerie;
    Dull is the mornin; an cheerless the day.

Dear is the hawthorn where lastly we parted;
    An dear is the burnie that sings thro the glen;
But dearer to me is the youth of my bosom,
    That's found a far grave o'er the watery main.

Restless I roam, while the tempest is gathering,
    On dark floating clouds as they usher the gloom;
Fortune, I fear not they smiles nor thy frowning,
    Nought now can move me on this side the tomb

Song on the Abdication of Bonaparte*
Tune *"Willie was a wanton wag"*

Now blushing Spring in maiden pride,
    From Surly Winter wins the day;
Love trims his bow-string by her side,
    And tunes his universal lay.
The birken bush, the balmy dawn,
    Are sweet and mild, and fair to see;
But dearer far to captive man,
    Are Peace and Health, and Liberty.

Fell war no more will thin the land
    With fiery brand and withering breath;
Peace waves around her magic wand,
    And breaks the instruments of death.
See, where the war-worn soldiers come,
    Once more to view their native plains!
With joy they hail their friends - their home,
    And bless the hands that burst their chains.

* *In the second edition the title read "Song on the Prospect o Peace"*

Let BOURBON lilies lift their head,
    And spread their blossoms to the day!
The Red Rose round its odour shed,
    And let the harp of ERIN play!
SCOTIA, bring thou thy symbol forth!
    What though thy crest's but hamely gear,
The hardy Thistle of the North
    Has oft times stemmed the tide of weir!

Now well may Pride her lesson learn,
    And dread a brother's blood to spill; -
And well may all that Voice discern,
    Which bids the sons of men be still.
Yet though the proud, the great, is low,
    His eagles fall no more to rise -
We tread not on the vanquished foe,
    But learn by others to be wise.

Song for the North Briton's Society, Liverpool.
Tune *"Andrew wi his cutty Gun"*

November wins blaw loud and chill,
The bird chirms o'er the leafless tree;
The wintry blast is comin fast,
And loudly roars the restless sea:
    Yet blythe, blythe, and merry we'll be,
    Cauld and care we'll fling awa,
    This is but ae night in our lives,
    And wha could grudge though it were twa.

We're met to drink our mither's health,
Yon carlin by the heugh and cairn;
What though auld Scotland's hills be bleak,
She's fostered mony a wally bairn.
    Sae blythe, blythe and merry we'll be,
    Scotia's sons we're ane and a;
    This is, etc.

It makes na here for garb or gear,
We look to mind and manly worth;
Dishonour blast the pridefu wight,
Wha scorns his friens or land o birth:
    Dull, dull and dowie be he,
    Gout and vapours round him draw;
    Thus let him hoard his worthless wealth,
    And social mirth be far awa.

Far foreign climes may shew their vines,
Their myrtle bowers, or orange tree;
As proud our doughty thistle waves,
For Caledon has aye been free.
  Blythe, blythe and merry are we,
  Liberty's the best o't a,
  This is, etc.

Oh! leeze me on her lanely glens,
Where gushing floods roar o'er the linn;
Her greensward howes, and echoing shores,
Where pibrochs wake a glorious din.
  Blythe, blythe and halesome are they,
  Our ain strathspeys they best can blaw;
  This is, etc.

When gloamin spreads her sober grey,
By broomy Orr, or birken Dee,
Sic scenes can soothe the festering mind,
Aboon a pleasures art can gie.
  Blythe, blythe and merry are we;
  The heart aye bows to nature's law;
  This is, etc.

England has daughters fair and gay,
Smooth, red and white, as maids need be;
But aft they want the native notes
And speaking glance o Leezie's ee.
  Blythe, blythe and bonny are they;
  Here's Scotlan's lasses ane and a;
  This is, etc.

Here's Byron's health, the chief o bards,
Here's Burns's memory (three times three),
Wi a the rest o tunefu train,
Frae Homer down to hamely me.
    Blythe, blythe and merry were they;
    Fill your glasses, toast them a;
    Unto the last night o our lives
    We winna let their memory fa.

The Tailor Triumphant
Tune *"Quaker's Wife"*

I'm Tailor Tom, from London come,
    With all my cuts and capers;
I've fashions new, of every cue,
    Cut out on shreds of papers.
'Tis mighty strange how things will change!
    For sure I never dream'd on't,
To stitch or mope in country shop,
    Or ever chalk a seam in't.

[*Spoken* - Well, isn't that a great mark of condescension in a gentleman of my dress, figure, and appearance, to deny myself the pleasure of Stitch Street and Broker Lane, and to be slump't up with a set of clodhoppers (civilly speaking)? But I can assure you, it was merely for the discharge of my conscience at seeing your cloth so unfashionably cut, and for a new improvement upon the Ladies' - Tal the dall, lal etc.]

What would ye think, these hands of mine,
    Made drawers for a duchess;
Stitch'd ribbon-stars for dukes so fine,
    And brac'd a maid in breeches!
I've set a button on a suit,
    To grace a birth-day levee;
And cut for colonels in the ranks,
    And captains in the navy.

[*Spoken* - Gentlemen and Ladies, you may believe me, London's the place for honour and preferment. - Every man there is measured by his clothing. I've there known a drill-serjeant pass for a captain, a laird for a lord, a curate for a bishop, a French farrier for a graduate; - even I, myself, often for a man-milliner - but we never seem'd to know them in our shop; that is to say, if they pull'd freely, it made them contented, and us to sing, - Tal the dall, lal, etc.]

O! London fine, for ladies kind,
    Of every rank and station -
For belles and beaux, sure more it shows,
    Than any town i the nation.
'Twas on a night, when drest so tight,
    A doxy did salute me;
So kind and free she blink'd on me,
    And threw her arms about me.

[*Spoken* - Faith, and after all, I believe she made more free than welcome, for instead of hugging and squeezing me out of pure kindness, as I imagined, she hugged me out of a whole week's wages, my thimble, shears, and all the rest of my appendages, - leaving me idle, only with a bodkin wanting the point, to sing, - Tal the dall, lal, etc.]

A Tale of Terror

Yestreen, as I staw by yon auld ruined wa,
    Where heroes lie mouldering and rotten,
There the chieftain of fame, and the fair peerless dame,
    Lie low in their mansion, forgotten.

Below yon grey stanes lie the friar's haly banes,
    And the nun's in yon mouldering cloister,
That lived their chaste lives without husbands or wives,
    Wi pains and wi penance right austere.

Now lowly ye rest; but your sauls they are blest;
    For honour and truth was your treasure:
And ye holy few, that, secluded frae view,
    Despising each wordly pleasure.

Thus musing I strode o'er the green grassy sod,
    And thought on the frailties o nature,
How man's like a flower, that's cut down in an hour:
    A weak, thoughtless, short-sighted creature.

Midnight came soon, and the pale waning moon
    O'er the verge her last shred was declining;
Dark clouds gathered roun with a dismal like gloom,
    As if spirits o darkness were joining.

The ominous note frae the raven's hoarse throat,
    Was joined by the far-flying heron;
Thro the vaults the wind sang, and the untouched bell rang,
    Chorused up by the owl's screeching clarion.

Loud the rain lashed frae the wings o the blast,
    And louder the thunder did bellow;
The lightning's rude dash o'er the ruins did flash,
    While demons of darkness did follow.

When lo! to the west, where the ivy had prest,
    Rose the moanings of misery and horror;
The fire-bas they fell, like red bolts shot frae hell,
    Spreading fear, devastation, and terror.

When near to yon bust raise twa knights frae the dust,
    Wha's looks teemed wi terror and vengeance:
Said, "Through fervent zeal we've our souls sent to hell,
    Beings of kings and of devils the engines.

Our arms we have strained for what fate ne'er ordained;
    For the tomb and yon temple sae bonny,
To clear Jewish parks frae Saracens and Turks,
    And become a Jerusalem Johnny.

"Thro the fray we have dash'd till our feet have been washed
    Wi blood o the innocent Persian;
But never yet deemed, while their bodies we seamed,
    That we from our duties were swerving.

"In our demon-like grup we have women ripped up,
    Though the child in the womb has been starting;
While the sum of our gains, and reward of our pains,
    Was the gift of a green or blue garten."

Then neist frae the groun, raise a friar and a nun,
    Twa spectres wi horrible grinnin,
They wildly accused, and each ither abused,
    For secretly tempting to sinnin.

"From the rich," says the monk, "I have eaten and drunk,
    And paid with a Pope's toleration;
I have taught them a lie, for which I now fry,
    And soothed o'er their souls to damnation.

"The poor I have racked till their heart-strings have cracked,
    Stained their daughters with guilt and infection:
I have lain with men's wives, challenged, then taen their lives,
    And all without dread of detection.

"Made religion a cloak, real piety a joke,
    And hatched conspiracy and treason;
And in prosperous days we made faggots to blaze,
    And curbed every dawning of reason."

"And me," said the nun, "you've for ever undone,
    By your lewd and your lawless caresses;
You strangled my child, though the innocent smiled;
    And laughed at a mother's distresses."

"You lie!" said the priest, anger swelled in his breast,
    "Thy child had a convent of fathers;
'Twas far other aims than confessing your sins,
    Made you twine round our bodies like adders.

"Thy dark hollow soul, with hypocrisy foul,
    Thou varlet - thou base lying Vandal!
What fiend ever matched ye false women debauched
    Ye caused me, to save you from scandal."

But the morning bell strook, when I backward did look,
    To muse on these prospects sae dreary;
There was nought I could view but the dark waving yew;
    Through the turrets the wind whistled eerie.

The Tear Hung in his Ee
Tune *"Logan Braes"*

Oh! pale, pale rose the April morn,
My sodger lad frae me was torn;
Then honour's name was hard to dree;
The parting tear hung in his ee.
But loud the pealing trumpet sang,
And loud the warlike cymbals clang;
Then honour's fause name ruined me,
Although the love- tear blint his ee.

'Twas no his locks of amber brown,
His manly limbs in armour bound;
His graceful snawie archèd brow,
His dimpled cheek sae sweet to view;
Nor buddin lips that gae delight,
Half shieldin teeth of ivory white;
But 'twas his glance that ruined me,
The lovely language o his ee.

Now he has found a foreign grave,
Far, far ayont the roaring wave,
Within yon luckless ravaged land,
Wi thousands on Corunna's strand.
In fancying sleep, how aft I've seen
His rising grave that grows sae green,
Then starting, waked wi tearfu ee;
For Oh! he's cauld and far frae me.

Nae mair the flowers in wreaths we'll twine,
Wi which my brows he used to bin;
Nae gay attire my breast can ease;
Alas! there's nane I wish to please!
Though sair's my heart, I loe the pain,
And sweet's the tear that's shed alane;
And dear's the pledge he gae to me,
That day the tear hung in his ee.

To Tobacco

Foul fa thee, vile unchancie docken,
That e'er thou set thy neb in Scotlan;
For now, 'tween sneezin, chowin, smokin,
   There's few are free;
And 'tweel thy taste's no sae provokin,
   'Tween you and me.

Nae doubt, like ither tares o evil,
Ye've first been dibbled by the devil:
Although ye look sae simply civil,
   Yet aft 'tis thee
Joins tattlin jades in clubs convivial,
   To clash and lie.

When autumn, wi yer yellow tap,
Sits bendin ripe in Nature's lap,
And farmers, keen to cut the crap,
   Lest wins should scud it,
Yet weary wives roun coals will clap,
   By thee deludit.

Last year, ere Meg began a-spinnin
Her lang projected wab o linen,
To light her pipe she thought nae sin in -
   Teazin her tow;
Countin wi care her costs and winnin,
   The stock took low!

Our auld gudeman, sae crouse and canty,
That said his prayers like ony saint aye,
Tinin his spleuchan i the pantry -
       Now frets and granes,
And banns, and glowers, and girns, and gaunts aye,
       And paiks the weans.

When bairns and auld folks gang to rest,
And youngsters roun the fire are placed,
Ilk ane sits neist wha he likes best,
       Amang the kimmers,
To read their fortune's kittle cast,
       Amang the emers.

Then Pate pus out his sneeshin-mill,
And Peg will hae't again his will,
While she, poor young thing, deems nae ill -
       He darklins grips her:
Some luckless creepie hits her heel,
       And backward trips her.

Yestreen, while smokin by the hallan,
Blythe Bess cam by the sonsie callan,
I fain my chin her cheek wad hauled on -
       But nae remead -
She said my breath was past a tholin:
       O! cursed weed.

Thou picklest aft the poor man's penny;
Ye shake the nerves o waefu grannie:
'Tis thee maks monie a thriftless mammie,
      And loiterin dad;
And spoils the bluid o' Kate and Annie,
      Till beauties fade.

Thou feed'st a batch o idle loons,
O chapmen chiels in borough towns;
And cursed excisemen gaun their rouns,
      Wi saucy gnash;
Forbye a batch o spinster clowns,
      And sic like trash.

Wae worth the man first brought you here!
Freedom appalled, looks back wi fear,
Where cowerin wretches do you rear,
      Baith air and late;
And stifle sorrow's briny tear,
      In slavery's state.

Had ye been meant for Scotlan's gude,
To clear the min, or clean the bluid,
Ayont the sea ye wadna stood
      Where ye're a weed o;
For she supplies ilk herb and food,
      That we hae need o.

But now, we're sae far seen in arts,
And learned the gate to foreign parts,
That countra clauchans now are marts
        For foreign dainties;
We've lost our strength and honest hearts,
        Sin ye cam sklent us.

Awa ye foreign jaups and gills,
Ye've brought auld Scotlan mony ills;
Her bairns torn down, wi puffs and pills,
        Tryin to mend them,
Till, totterin through her heath clad hills
        Ye'd hardly ken them:

A poor, degenerate pigmy race,
Wi tame dependence in their face,
Puffed up wi pride and pert grimace,
        Powdered and frizzed -
Strut turkey-like frae place to place,
        Half dead, half crazed!

O, for the days when Wallace bled,
And Scotlan's sons to glory led;
Or when Bruce drew the martial blade,
        At Bannockburn:
But, ah, alas! thae days are fled,
        Ne'er to return.

Let English dine on pork and pease;
Let Welshmen plot and toast their cheese,
Gie Boney paddock fricasees,
      And fish to Dutchmen -
But brose, and hame-brewed barley-brees,
      Can rear the Scotchman.

Verses
added to Burns's "Over the Forth"

His face like the morn, or the rose newly blown,
      His hair like the blackbird that skims o'er the lee;
His person is fine, an his heart it is kin,
      An sweet is the blink o his dark rollin ee.

But where shall I find ought to figure his mind,
      Or equal his valor or true love to me;
But his fortune was hard, an his friens broke their word,
      That has forcd him to leae his dear baby an me.

What thoughts did I feel when he bade me fareweel,
      While the grief partin tear it did start in our ee;
How my heart it did beat when I view'd the sad fate,
      That tore him for ay frae his ain country.

Now day gies nae joy but to gaze on my boy,
      An night brings nae comfort but tears to my ee;
In sorrow I'll mourn, for he ne'er can return;
      Far far does he roam frae his baby an me.

Verses on a Cottage in Ruins

Hail! peace to your mansions, where Ruin has ravaged,
    Your low strawy roof, now fallen to decay;
Your thresholds untrod, there the green grass is waving:
    Your walls they are mouldered, and naked, and grey.
Thus Time doth dissect, with calm deliberation
    Enfeebled's thy form by each blast that doth blow;
And savage, and sage, the proud prince and the peasant,
    And heroes, and empires, like thee are laid low.

Here sat the fond housewife and parent united,
    While Virtue's plain precepts oft flowed from her tongue;
Now silence reigns round, save the Dee's lonely murmurs,
    Or the wail of the night-bird bereft of her young.
The hawthorn blooms grey - the trees spread their branches;
    The primrose has blossomed - yet nought can avail,
No rustic returns with his song in the evening -
    No fond lovers meet now to breathe the soft tale.

Where are the youngsters with gambol and frolic?
    In life's early morn, light they trod the flowered green;
Each sod, seat, and path, the rude plough has defacëd,
    And nettles and wild weeds luxuriant are seen.
Perhaps, like their cottage, unpitied, unenvied,
    They silently sleep the cold green sod below;
Or fettered by gain, strive to win the gold anchor,
    On fortune's rude tide, through a world full of woe.

No more shall the stranger, when wearied and worn,
  Find shelter to shield him with comfort or rest;
In thy mansions, though low, have the naked been clothëd,
  And soothed the sunk heart of the lonely distrest.
Here science might shine like the flower in the desert,
  And mild meditation her vigils prolong;
Still, such are the scenes where the muse loves to wander,
  And weave her lone thoughts in the heart-soothing song.

Verses on the Death of a Dairymaid

The dawn of the morning had spread o'er the sky,
  And the curling mists waved o'er the sea,
The breath of the breeze to the mountains passed by,
  And the dew spangles hung on the tree,

As lonely I strayed by yon briar-feathered brake,
  Pleased the rude draughts of Nature to view,
Or watched the wild waterfowl skim o'er the lake,
  Where the flower of the wilderness grew.

Thus oft have I marked, even in Poverty's shade,
  The cottage of Peace to adorn,
The mild timid looks of the young village maid,
  As the primrose peeps out by the thorn.

Oh! emblem of innocence! modest and mild,
  And pure as the dews on thy breast;
Thus bloomed thou, ELIZA - thus sweetly thou smiled -
  Ere thou sunk to thy cold bed of rest.

I've heard when thy notes through the dairy were rung,
 With the laugh and the jest oft between -
I've seen when the mower his scythe lighter swung,
 As thou turn'dst up the swaird on the green.

No more shall that eye now be lighted by love -
 How changed is its lustre and hue!
And fled every charm the dull hermit might move -
 But 'tis painful the contrast to view.

Yet did not the blossoms that bloomed on thy cheek,
 Speak of years yet unnumbered to run?
And did not thy dreams, in futurity, seek
 For new joys yet unruffled to come?

But where are the lovers that worshipped those eyes,
 And vowed every frown was despair? -
As the light-feathered emigrant woos other skies,
 So they follow where summer blooms fair.

Save one pensive youth, by yon pine-covered steep,
 While the blast through the branches does moan,
He sighs there in secret, he mourns while asleep,
 And he loves to be always alone.

No youthful companion can soften his grief,
 Nor friend bear a part in his pain;
But he turns his dim eye on the sear-withered leaf,
 And he weeps - and then views it again.

Poor mourner - thy moments how seldom now sweet?
 But the darkest night yields to the day:
Hope points to the time when true lovers will meet,
 And thy tears shall be all wiped away.

Verses on the Death of a Young Woman
Written on the 31st December, 1821

'Tis sweet at sober eve to walk,
    To hear the leaves fall from the trees;
To see the foxglove's withered stalk
    Bend with December's latest breeze!

Each busy haunt of men is still;
    (Oh! could the mind thus rest from care!)
The bird sleeps on the wooded hill,
    The beasts have found their wonted lair.

The blustering chilly winds are laid;
    The waning moon peers thin and pale;
The streamlet tinkles o'er its bed,
    And slowly winds along the vale.

Yon spangles of the clear blue sky,
    Now shed their light on all below;
They charm our thoughts to soar on high,
    Yet teach how little man can know.

The Sun, in all his glory bright,
    Gives light; and life, and form, and hue;
But see! the grey-clad matron, Night;
    Brings worlds unnumbered to our view.

What are we in creation's scale?
    How should we act? Who sent us here?
Let calm reflection lift the veil,
    And welcome in the infant year.

Another annual round has passed,
     Another glass old Time has run;
Pale Memory fears to view the last,
     While Reason asks, "What have ye done?"

We little think, while health attends,
     How unperceived youth glides away;
The longest term that life extends,
     When past, seems but a winter day.

Our toils, our joys, our anxious fears,
     Have with the seasons come and gone,
But some have left this world of cares
     To sleep, "unnoticed and unknown."

Oh, Is'bel! all thy pains are past:
     Thy tender voice no more I hear;
Like distant music on the blast,
     It fell upon my ravished ear.

Alas! thou shar'st not now my care,
     Nor mark'st the sigh, nor tears I shed;
For dim's thine eye, and dull's thine ear,
     Even Sorrow's voice wakes not the dead.

Thy anxious, young, inquiring mind,
     Thy slender form, and pensive eye;
Thy gentle spirit, true and kind -
     Sure so much goodness could not die!

Know'st thou a friend or lover's woe?
    See'st thou mute Nature, reft and bare?
Canst thou each earthly tie forego?
    Where is thy dwelling - tell me where?

Perhaps thy pure and hallowed shade
    Is hovering round with guardian power,
To yield, unseen, thy friendly aid
    And comfort at this midnight hour.

Even now, methinks, some healing balm
    Steals through my shattered languid frame;
My broken spirit feels a calm,
    While whispering breezes breathe thy name.

But why should feeble Fancy rove
    Beyond the reach of mortal ken?
Or seeks the prying eye of Love,
    What Heaven has hid from sons of men?

Soon shall we mingle side by side;
    The young, the old, soon follow you:
Well! if the Golden Rule's our guide,
    We need not fear what Death can do!

Verses to a Fly

Fluttering insect of a day,
Gaily you your wings display;
Lightly you traverse your round
O'er the flower-enamelled ground;
Or buzz beneath the hazel shade,
With primrose pale, and violet spread;
By gushing stream, or dimpling pool,
Where yielding air is soft and cool,
Unmindful of the trout beneath,
That lurks in ambush for your death:
Or subtle spider on the brow,
That weaves the web of fate for you -
Where, lawyer-like, he spreads his gin,
To draw the gay and thoughtless in.
    See ye not yon gloomy west,
Where lowering clouds the sky o'ercast?
There distant darkness dims the plain,
Prophetic of approaching rain;
Or chilling blast, with hailstones fraught,
Might murder myriads in a thought,
And dash your being, and your name,
To barren nought, from whence ye came:
Nor leave a mourner to relate,
Or sing a brother's hapless fate.
    Yet still ye wheel, and still ye sing,
On fluttering pleasure's airy wing,
Unconscious of your shortlived power,
That stints your being to an hour.
Alas! your sight, so quick and clear,
Views but the objects that are near.
Your convex eye, that's made to view

Each film, and wing, and form, and hue
Of atoms, insects, nicely made,
From eager poring Science hid;
But leaves unnoticed hills and towers,
And clouds, and skies, and coming showers.
With forethought shorter than your sight,
Fearless ye urge your aerial flight,
As lightly round the dance ye wheel
Of life's fantastic fairy reel.
But when the thread of life is spun,
Your debts are paid, your work is done.

      So fares the beauteous, hapless maid,
Tutored in flattery's empty shade,
While youthful blossoms paint her form,
She sees not ruin's ruthless storm;
How soon her thread of pleasure's spun,
And ends ere life has well begun!
Some callous wretch, of reptile kind,
Destroys her peace, and taints her mind;
Whose poisonous tongue's with flattery oiled,
But leaves her when her rose is soiled.

      Thus fares the Poet and his lays,
If Fame - the sunshine of his days -
Beam brisk, like thee, he'll mount and sing,
On soaring Fancy's airy wing;
And *ignis fatuus*-like he'll shine,
While swains for him the laurels twine;
Till critics all his lines dissect,
And damn his works with disrespect.
Adieu! his sanguine hopes are fled;
His name is in oblivion dead.

      'Tis thus, if human life we view -
The picture's too severely true;
Though armed with reason's piercing eye,

Too oft we ape the silly fly;
Till lawless passions empire claim,
And damn our souls, and blot our fame.

Verses on Seeing a Domesticated Goat

Tenant of the mountain's brow!
    Why thus thy youthful haunts forsake?
With shaggy garb of snowy hue,
    Thou seek'st a shade by wood and brake;
There, thoughtless crop'st the flowery swaird,
With warrior front, and hermit beard.

Thou mind'st no more the rude grey cairn,
    Where awful Silence slumbering lies,
Nor dark caves, crowned with heath and fern,
    That echoed back thy mother's cries.
The scene how wild! yet, oh, how grand!
Who robbed thee of thy birthright? Man.

For thee no female trims her hair,
    Nor offspring round thee gambols play;
No rival comes, with threatening air,
    Thy hidden valour to display:
Thy life's unvaried, dull and tame;
Thus bound and shackled stains thy name.

So Liberty, the mountain maid,
    On Scotia's cliffs once tuned her strains,
Till taught with gems her hair to braid,
    To sing and toy with southern swains;
Her freeborn spirit soon was broke -
She bows 'neath Luxury's golden yoke.

The Wild Wood-Side
Tune *"Ballochmyle"*

Alone I walked the wild wood-side,
    Where Autumn breathed her airy breeze;
The silver moon-shine, far and wide,
    Beamed glimmering through the branching trees.
The birdies now, on leafless bough,
    Their carols gay had laid aside;
Grave silence reigns through woods and plains
    With me along the wild wood-side.

Far-roaring Dee burst o'er his rocks,
    While distance tuned his swelling moans,
O'erhung with oak, and ivied locks,
    Where owls screeched out their wailing tones.
The fragrant bean was withering seen,
    And flowery hawthorn's bloom decayed;
No heavenly dew shall them renew,
    Till Spring revive the wild wood-side.

Now sleep her patent spell hath drawn,
    And charmed creation into rest,
Save only thoughtless, hapless man,
    Where guilt or love disturbs the breast.
Sweet Peace! descend, be thou my friend,
    And white-robed Innocence my guide;
And teach me clear my course to steer,
    Poor wanderer by the wild wood-side.

Ye twinkling stars, that shine afar,
    To me unknown's your distant race -
Ye comets on your fiery car,
    That wander through the boundless space -
Can Science scan your voice to man,
    As through the concave blue ye glide,
And teach such views to vagrant muse,
    That wanders by the wild wood-side?

Where now the distant landscape sweet?
    Where now the busy haunts of men?
The chill dews o'er the grey grass creep,
    The reapers now have left the plain.
With every blast the leaves fall fast,
    As down the stream they mournful ride,
Changed Nature here looks pale and drear,
    With me along the wild woods

Again the lamp of day shall burn;
    With harmony the woods shall ring;
The annual wheel of time shall turn,
    With all the rosy hues of Spring:
But Man, when laid in lonely bed,
    His griefs and joys are laid aside;
He ne'er again shall view the plain,
    Or beauties of the wild wood-side.

Will and Kate
or, an answer to "Logan Braes"

Thou maid, that sing'st by Logan stream,
Wi plaintive note, and pensive mien,
While true affection tunes thy lays,
For thy ain lad on Logan braes,
As yon sweet linnet, in the spring,
Teaches her chirpin young to sing,
So thou, wi thine, may'st con thy waes -
He'll ne'er see thee, nor Logan braes.

For oh! what bosom without pain,
Can tell our sad mishaps in Spain? -
He's fan, wi Moore, o deathless praise,
Far, far frae thee and Logan braes.
Wi sleepless nights, and famine faint,
Fell numbers urged him frae his tent;
Yet aft he, wheelin, faced his faes,
And thought on thee, and Logan braes.

But ere the fatal die was cast,
I saw him nobly breathe his last. -
"Gae, tak that ring," he faintly says,
"And bear't to Kate, on Logan braes."
The deadly tale her heart will stound -
But ebbin life gushed frae ilk wound:
His latest accents spoke thy praise,
And blest his babes on Logan braes.

Hae ye no seen the Autumn flower
Bow down its head wi e'enin shower,
Till chillin frost its form bewrays,
And lays it low on Logan braes?
She beat her breast - her hans she rung;
Her hapless younglins round her clung;
What pen, alas! can paint her waes?
She's faintin, fan on Logan braes.

But lo! the sodger doft his arms;
Like lightnin, clasped her fleeting charms -
Says, "Ope thine eyes of kindest rays
On thy ain lad on Logan braes."
These accents kind her spirits cheer;
She views her lad wi joyfu tear:
Wi joy they press - wi joy they gaze,
And kiss their babes on Logan braes.

"Oh! dearest Kate, can ye forgie
The absent years I've been frae thee?"
Then in her lap a purse he lays,
That he'd brought hame to Logan braes. -
Says, - "This shall help for what is gane,
And I'll ne'er leave thee mair thy lane;
While life-blood in my bosom plays,
I'll stay wi thee on Logan braes.

"Ilk flutterin bird mair sweet shall sing;
Ilk blushin flower mair sweet shall spring;
Our bairns shall herd, and gather slaes
Aroun our cot, on Logan braes.
To each fond haunt we will repair,
Where I'll tell o'er my deeds o weir;
While the blythe lambkin round us plays,
And pipes sound shrill on Logan braes."

On Youthful Hope

Oh! Hope, thou cheat'st the young and gay,
    Wi fondest expectation;
For pleasin Fancy paints the way
    Without investigation.

Alas! thou little ken'st the care
    O thorny life's employment;
Thy fairy figures promise fair,
    But tine in the enjoyment.

Yet when I think on days that's by,
    How happy ye hae made me,
I fin my heart aft heave the sigh,
    That e'er ye should hae fled me.

What gars ye, waverin, smilin Hope,
    And fickle Fancy, leae me?
For Reason, wi his boasted prop,
    But little comfort gies me.

He's but a paughty sullen guide,
    His paths are no aye pleasin;
And then the heart-strings downa bide
    Gin e'er a body leaes him:

And wardly Wisdom, wi her wiles,
    Keeps aye a body waukin;
She clogs the mind wi care and toils,
    For either thought or talkin.

Come, Fancy wi thy magic skill,
    And wrap me in Elysium;
Though ye're the elder sister still,
    Ye never fail to please ane.

But cankered Care's taen up the min,
    Without an invitation, -
Will keep his haud, till made to tine,
    By Time his eerie station.

What art thou, restless, woefu wight,
    That wring'st the heart unceasin?
That wounds the mind, and wrecks the sight
    Wi thoughts and views unpleasin? -

That's ever waukin; aye at wark,
    Although we canna see thee;
Gropin for something in the dark,
    The warld canna gie thee?

O Hope, come wi thy shinin power,
    Anchor my thoughts, and right me,
Afore the dark and dreary hour
    Of dread despair benight me!

ACKNOWLEDGEMENTS

The collection would not have been possible without the invaluable assistance of many people. Dr David Devereux of the Stewartry Museum, Kirkcudbright, first roused my interest in matters of local literary history. He has remained committed in his support and assistance and made the museum library available whenever I wanted it. Another special mention needs to be made of Broughton House, the former home of artist E A Hornel in Kirkcudbright's High Street, now in the care of the National Trust for Scotland. Jim Allan, the Librarian, and Frances Scott, manager of Broughton House, enabled me to bring to publication two previously unpublished works and provided much biographical information on Nicholson. Support for the project has come from many quarters and I have to thank Alastair Johnson, director of Dumfries and Galloway Library Service, who has always supported my desire to get Nicholson's work across to the public. Wigtown Book Town, and particularly Mr Roy Surplice and Mr Ian Barr, was invaluable to this particular edition, and their faith in local literary matters is exemplary. A mention, too, must go to Janet Smyth and Readiscovery in Edinburgh who published the National Poetry Day Postcard in 1998 featuring an excerpt from Nicholson's "Brownie of Blednoch". John Carter took on the burden of publishing this volume and so without him the whole venture would have foundered. Then there has been the inspirational support from Mr Tony Bonning whose rendering of "The Brownie of Blednoch" and "The Braes of Galloway" is today spoken of whenever the name of William Nicholson is mentioned locally. To name one more inspiration, Mr Alexander Allan of Carse, Kirkcudbright, has always been diligent in his theories over the life and times of one of Galloway's greatest native poets. But that is only the beginning. The Kirkcudbright Poetry Class that meets on

Monday evenings has helped with many issues of pronunciation and contacts. Local historians have taken time to do research that I simply didn't have the means to undertake. Thanks too, to Mr Robert Mitchell, for the wonderful John Faed drawing that graces this edition. Finally, to name a moving spirit that introduced me to the name of William Nicholson, I'd like to say thank you to poet and friend, Mr Donald Adamson, who spends most of his time in Finland these days but who is fondly remembered by all writers living in Galloway.

The Local History Series

This series of books is being published in order to satisfy the ever increasing interest in the history of Galloway, especially the county of Wigtownshire.

It is our intention to continue to publish further titles indefinitely as and when they are ready for printing.

Some of the books will be previously unpublished material. As such they will be in great demand by local historians, educationalists and libraries along with the "man in the street".

No 1	"Pigot's Directory of Wigtownshire 1837"	£3.00
No 4	"The Mulberry Harbour Project in Wigtownshire" 2nd ed.	£5.95
No 5	"Pigot's Directory of Kirkcudbrightshire 1837"	£3.00
No 6	"Pigot's Directory of Dumfriesshire 1837"	£4.50
No 7	"Pigot's Directory of Ayrshire 1837"	£6.50
No 8	"Albanich - The History of the Galloway Rifles"	£28.50
No 9	"History of Sorbie Parish Church"	£3.00
No 12	"Ruby - Life in Galloway & Glasgow"	£3.00
No 13	"Lands & Their Owners in Galloway" 5 vols., 2500pp hd. bk. in cloth	£100.00
No 14	"Highways & Byways in Galloway"	Out of print
No 15	"The Persecutions in Scotland, 1605 - 1685"	£4.00
No 16	"Reminiscences of Wigtonshire" Samuel Robinson	£10.95
No 17	"A Sailor Boy's Experience" Samuel Robinson	£12.95
No 18	"The Lost Railways of Galloway"	£4.00
No 20	"The Lost Railways of Ayrshire"	£5.95
No 21	"Cairn Ryan Military Port - A History"	£6.95
No 22	"Penninghame - The Story of a Parish"	£16.95
No 23	"Exploring Galloway - A Series of Sixteen Historical Walks"	£6.45
No 24	"RAF in Galloway" second edition	available Autumn '99
No 25	"William Nicholson - The Bard of Galloway"	£6.95
No 26	"The House that Sugar Built"	available Summer '99

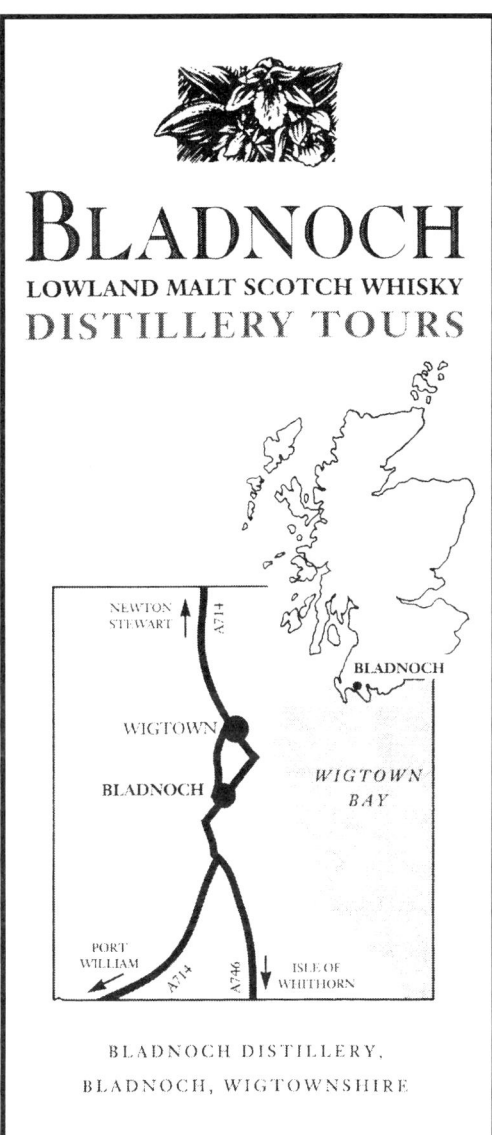

BLADNOCH

LOWLAND MALT SCOTCH WHISKY

DISTILLERY TOURS

BLADNOCH DISTILLERY,
BLADNOCH, WIGTOWNSHIRE

7 miles south of Newton Stewart and 40 minutes drive from the ferries to Ireland, is situated Scotland's most southerly distillery dating from 1817. A fine stone and slate building with it's attractive pagoda tower, it displays even today the skills of the original stonemasons.

This year the vast wooden wash backs and gleaming copper stills, silent since 1993 will once again produce the clear spirit of this unique Lowland Malt.

Have a guided tour and sample a complimentary dram. Browse in one of this areas best gift shops, with its excellent range of quality Scottish woolens and large selection of fine malt whiskys.

Relax, bring a picnic (indoor and outdoor area) or take a stroll up the iver, through Cotland Wood with its rare orchids, the logo of Bladnoch Single Malt.

Bladnoch Distillery, Bladnoch, Scotland, DG8 9AB

Open Monday-Friday 9.30 - 4.30 p.m.
Other times by appointment. Group visits,
Please arrange in advance by telephoning:

01988 402605 - off season tel. 018206 22842